WITNESS LEE

A Living of Mutual Abiding with the Lord in Spirit

Living Stream Ministry
Anaheim, CA

First Edition, January 2000.

ISBN 0-7363-0806-7

Published by

Living Stream Ministry
2431 W. La Palma Ave., Anaheim, CA 92801 U.S.A.
P. O. Box 2121, Anaheim, CA 92814 U.S.A.

Printed in the United States of America

00 01 02 03 04 05 / 9 8 7 6 5 4 3 2 1

CONTENTS

PREFACE

This book is composed of messages given by Brother Witness Lee in the Chinese-speaking meetings in Anaheim, California on the Lord's Days from June 26 through August 21, 1983. The messages were not reviewed by the speaker.

CHAPTER ONE

BORN TO LIVE

Scripture Reading: John 1:1, 4a, 12-13; 3:5-6, 14-15; 6:57, 63; 10:10b; 11:25a; 14:19b-20; 20:22; Rev. 1:18a

THE BIBLE BEING A BOOK OF LIFE

In this series of messages we want to see the believers' living of a mutual abiding with the Lord in spirit. Many people, including Christians, have an ingrained religious concept regarding the Bible. They think that the Bible is a book of religious teachings. Since every religion has its book of religious teachings, it seems Christianity also has its book, which is the Bible. It may seem so, but actually it is not. In reality the Bible is entirely a book on life, and this life which is referred to in the Bible is the Triune God as our life.

I have been speaking for the Lord for over fifty years. At the time I was saved I did not pay much attention to this life, so I began by spending about seven years to diligently study the Bible and other spiritual publications. This certainly influenced me very much inwardly and caused me to be constituted with many doctrines. Thus, when I rose to speak for the Lord after those seven or eight years, the emphasis of most of my speaking was on doctrines. However, gradually the desire for mere doctrines began to diminish, because after much speaking I no longer liked or was willing to speak them, and I even lost the taste for doctrines. From then on, my speaking began to shift toward life. After I turned to life, the more I spoke, the richer and more living my speaking became; the more I spoke, the more I enjoyed speaking and the more my speaking became inexhaustible. The result was that I then saw that all of the speaking in the Bible is life. Finally,

I saw that at the beginning of the Bible and at the end of the Bible there is a tree of life. In the first two chapters of the Bible, in the book of Genesis, we see that God created the heavens and the earth, and He created man. Then He put the man in front of the tree of life. This indicates that God's goal for man was that he be able to gain the life of this tree.

The life of the tree of life in the Bible is truly a mystery. What actually is the tree of life? Today there are some so-called Bible scholars who say that the tree of life is too ancient and has ceased to exist. This is not scriptural. The Bible shows us that not only in the beginning of time was there the tree of life, but even in eternity future there will still be the tree of life. In the book of Revelation, the tree of life is mentioned at least two or three times. In 2:7 the Lord said, "To him who overcomes, to him I will give to eat of the tree of life, which is in the Paradise of God." Chapter twenty-two says that in the middle of the street in the city of the New Jerusalem is a river of water of life and on either side of the river is the tree of life (vv. 1-2). This shows us that the tree of life is not very tall, but it does span both banks of the river. It is not a huge cedar but a vine that continues to spread out, and it is for man's supply, not something to be used as material. This tree of life grows alongside the river of life, and with the watering of the flow of the river it supplies life to people. This is truly an eternal blessing. At the end of Revelation 22, it says, "Blessed are those who wash their robes that they may have right to the tree of life" (v. 14). It is evident that the tree of life has not passed away but continues to exist and will continue unto eternity.

Not only so, the tree of life is here today. Revelation 2:7 says, "To him who overcomes, to him I will give to eat of the tree of life, which is in the Paradise of God." This does not point only to the future but refers to today. Whoever overcomes today, to him is the enjoyment of the tree of life, which is in the Paradise of God. What does this mean? If you have a bird's-eye view of the entire Bible, you will see that this tree of life is a figure that signifies, symbolizes, God Himself as our life. The Gospel of John says that the Lord Jesus is life and that He is also a tree, the true vine (14:6; 15:1). We know that a vine is not like a pine tree or a cedar tree for the producing of building materials. No one would use a grapevine to construct houses or furniture. The Lord Jesus said that He is life. He also said that He is the vinetree. When you put these two sentences together, you can see that He is the tree of life. Furthermore, according to its natural function, the vine is for the supply of life.

What the Bible tells us is that this Triune God has become our tree of life and that He is the source of the supply of life. Not only so, according to the revelation in the Bible, God ordained that everyone must have two births: to be born once of the mother's womb and once of God. In John 3, the Lord Jesus told Nicodemus, "Unless one is born of water and the Spirit, he cannot enter into the kingdom of God. That which is born of the flesh is flesh, and that which is born of the Spirit is spirit" (vv. 5-6). This tells us that God requires us to be born twice: once of the flesh and once of the Spirit. The first time is from the mother's womb; the second time is not to re-enter the mother's womb and come out again, but it is to be born of the Spirit. That which is born of our parents is of the flesh, just as the Lord said that that which is born of the flesh is flesh. We were all born of the flesh so that we can exist in this world. If you know the Bible and see God's arrangement, then you will see that God wants to have Himself born in us. Today God is the Spirit. God being born in us is the Spirit being born in us. We all have been born of the Spirit; this is to be born not of blood but of the Spirit.

MAN HAVING A SPIRIT TO RECEIVE GOD AS LIFE

An ancient Chinese sage said that man is the spirit of all creation. The reason man is precious, valuable, and wonderful is that there is a spirit in man. If the spirit of man were to be removed from man, he would be no different from the cats and dogs. Man is different from the beasts in that man has a spirit and the beasts do not. Throughout the ages you cannot find cats and dogs anywhere that have the desire to worship God. Nevertheless, human beings, whether civilized or barbarian, all have a desire to worship God. The barbarians have their crude method of worship; the civilized ones have their cultured way. The demonic gods that the backward nations worship are rough and wild; the idols that the civilized nations worship are rather refined. Why must man worship? The reason is that man has a spirit within which only God can satisfy. Even the atheistic Communists worship something. They worship themselves; their self is their god. The Bible says that with some their god is their stomach (Phil. 3:19). There is not one person who does not desire God; everyone wants God. Just as everyone has a stomach that requires food, so man has a spirit that requires the worship of God. Whether the god which man worships is true or false, refined or barbaric, the fact that man worships God proves that man has a spirit. God created man with a spirit, and this spirit has a need for God.

The spirit of man is for man to be regenerated. Our flesh is born of our parents, but God created us with a spirit that we may be born again. This is what it means to receive God into us. To be regenerated is to receive God into us. God is life. When we receive God into us, this God who is life enters into our spirit to be our life. According to Romans, we human beings are vessels (9:21) with an inner receiving organ for us to receive God. This is just like our stomach, which is a receiving organ to take in food. God is Spirit, and He created us with a spirit, which is the receiving organ for us to receive God. By using this spirit we receive God.

The Bible is not what most of us think it to be, a book of religious teachings or religious regulations. Rather, this Bible is a book of revelation, revealing God to man that man may know God as life. God created a spirit for man so that his spirit could take God in to be his life. If a man is willing to receive God into him to be his life, he will be regenerated in his spirit. This is the second birth. If you do not have the second birth, then you are incomplete, not up to par; you have not reached the standard. That God wants to be born in you is not a superstition but a fact. It is a fact that you have a spirit within. It is also a fact that God is Spirit. God is not only God but also life, which is the Spirit (John 4:24; 1 Cor. 15:45b). He is such a life-giving Spirit waiting for you to repent, confess, and open up yourself to receive the Lord Jesus to be your

Savior. The Lord Jesus is the life-giving Spirit. When you receive Him, you receive God, and He enters into you to be your life. Then you are regenerated and have another life within. This life is not only a higher life but also a superior life, the eternal life of God. This is the revelation of the entire Bible.

THE SUBJECT OF THE GOSPEL OF JOHN
BEING BORN TO LIVE

In the sixty-six books of the Bible, there is one book, the Gospel of John, which focuses on the matter of life. Most people when reading the Gospel of John tend to see only the superficial matters. In reality the emphasis of the Gospel of John is not on the outward things but on the matter of being born to live. Being born to live means that after one is born one must live. After we have been regenerated, we must live. If a person has not yet believed, or has not yet been saved, then he must be born again. The Gospel of John focuses on the matter of being born to live. In John 3, the Lord Jesus told Nicodemus that he must be born again and that he must be born of water and the Spirit. He also said, "That which is born of the Spirit is spirit" (v. 6). Later the Lord Jesus said, "Because I live, you also shall live," and "He who eats Me, he also shall live because of Me" (14:19; 6:57). In the Gospel of John you can see these two words: *born* and *live*. After you are born, you begin to live. You must not only be born, but you must also live.

John 1:1-2 says, "In the beginning was the Word, and the Word was with God, and the Word was God." Then it says, "In Him was life" (v. 4). This indicates that there is life in the Word. Since life is in Him, He is life. Then this Word who was in the beginning became flesh (v. 14), coming into mankind to reveal and explain Himself. Verses 12 and 13 say, "But as many as received Him, to them He gave the authority to become children of God, to those who believe into His name, who were begotten not of blood, nor of the will of the flesh, nor of the will of man, but of God."

If a person is willing to open to the Lord from his deepest part and say to the Lord, "Lord Jesus, I am a sinner. Lord, You are my Savior," then the Lord Jesus as the omnipresent Spirit will enter into him. I can truly testify that although I was born, raised, and even received my education in Christianity, I never really opened myself in this way to receive Jesus until the afternoon I heard the gospel. At that time I became deeply moved, and I opened up myself to receive the Lord. Once I received Him, I can truly testify that this Spirit entered into me and changed my whole life. Whoever receives Him, He will give him the authority to be a child of God. This authority is nothing other than the divine life. Because you have your father's life, you have the authority to be a child of your father. The authority to be the children of the father is the life of the father. Originally we did not have the authority to be the children of God, but after He put His life into us, we were born of Him and received the authority to be His children.

Then in John 3 we see that an elderly, moral man named Nicodemus came to see the Lord Jesus. The Lord Jesus said to him, "You must be born anew." Nicodemus thought this meant that he had to enter a second time into his mother's womb and be born; but the Lord Jesus seemed to be telling him, "No, because that which is born of the flesh is still flesh. You must be born again in spirit." In addition the Lord Jesus said, "As Moses lifted up the serpent in the wilderness, so must the Son of Man be lifted up, that every one who believes into Him may have eternal life" (vv. 14-15). This means that we humans were not only created but also bitten by the serpent, that is, poisoned by Satan. As a poisonous serpent, Satan bit us; hence, we received his poisonous element into us and became little poisonous serpents. Although Nicodemus was a just and upright man, perfect in his outward behavior, his inward nature was poisoned due to Satan's poisonous injection. Thus, what the Lord meant in speaking to Nicodemus was, "I must not only be a Lamb to die for you and make redemption for your sins, but I must also be a bronze serpent to deal with your serpentine nature. I must die in this way that you may be able to receive Me, believe into Me, and thereby obtain eternal life."

On the one hand, the Gospel of John tells us that as the

Lamb of God, the Lord Jesus took away the sin of the world; this is to deal with sin. On the other hand, it tells us that He was hung on the cross as the bronze serpent; this is to deal with the serpentine nature within us. The natural life within every one of us is serpentine. When the Lord Jesus died on the cross, He was not only the Lamb but also the bronze serpent. On the cross He died in the form of a serpent that on the one hand our sinful deeds might be dealt with by the Lamb and on the other hand our sinful nature within might be dealt with by the bronze serpent. The purpose for this is that whoever would believe into Him might receive eternal life.

After His death and resurrection, the Lord Jesus became the life-giving Spirit. First Corinthians 15:45b says, "The last Adam became a life-giving Spirit." Today Jesus Christ has risen from the dead, and in resurrection He is the life-giving Spirit. If you are willing to open yourself to believe into Him, believing that He died on the cross for your sin and sins and solved the problem of your sin and sins, then as the life-giving Spirit He will enter into you, and you will be regenerated.

In John 6 the Lord Jesus went on to say, "He who eats Me, he also shall live because of Me" (v. 57). This shows that today the resurrected Christ not only gives us life but also becomes our food. Genesis 1 tells us that God placed man in front of the tree of life that man might eat of it. From the word *eat* I found the key and gradually understood why in John 6 the Lord Jesus said that we need to eat Him. Thereafter, I began to release the truths on eating, drinking, and enjoying the Lord.

Today Christianity teaches people the Bible by treating it like a religious book. Actually, the words in the Bible are the words breathed out of the mouth of God. The Lord Jesus said, "Man shall not live on bread alone, but on every word that proceeds out through the mouth of God" (Matt. 4:4). Jeremiah also said, "Your words were found and I ate them" (Jer. 15:16). The Lord Jesus is edible; He said that He is our bread of life (John 6:35). The bread of life is for man to eat. In John 1 He is life, and in John 6 He is the bread of life. This is because between chapter one and chapter six there is regeneration.

After you are born, you must live, and to live you must eat. If you do not eat after your birth, you cannot stay alive.

Hence, the sequence in the Bible is very particular. Chapter one of the Gospel of John tells us that the Lord Jesus is life. Chapter three tells us that by this life we are regenerated. Then chapter six tells us that we must eat the Lord Jesus as the bread of life. John 6:63a says, "It is the Spirit who gives life." Because this phrase *who gives life* has a twofold meaning in Greek, a better rendering is: "who causes man to live and gives life to man." He not only gives life to man but also causes man to live; He not only causes man to live but also gives life to man. Both concepts are present; this phrase bears a twofold meaning. He who gives life to man and causes man to live is the Spirit. Then the Lord Jesus continued, "The words which I have spoken to you are spirit and are life" (v. 63b). We have the Spirit and the words. Praise the Lord, today we who are saved have the Lord Jesus as the Spirit within and the Bible as the words without! These two cannot be separated. The words without and the Spirit within must not be separated. The words without are not for teaching but for nourishment; likewise, the Spirit within is also for nourishment. Both are our food for our nourishment. Therefore, when we eat the Lord, we receive His words and allow His words to become the Spirit within. As a result, His words and the Spirit become our food and supply within.

Then in chapter ten, the Lord Jesus said, "I have come that they may have life and may have it abundantly" (v. 10b). To have life is to be regenerated; to have it more abundantly is to eat daily. To have life is to receive the Lord; to have it more abundantly is to eat the Lord daily, receive the word of the Lord daily, and touch the Spirit of the Lord daily through His word. In addition, the Lord said, "I am the resurrection and the life" (11:25a). Today we no longer live by our old life; instead, we live by another life, a regenerated life, a resurrected life. Then in 14:19b He said, "Because I live, you also shall live." According to the context, we can see that His living refers to His being resurrected. He seemed to be saying, "I am going now; the world will no longer see Me, but you will see Me soon; because I live, you shall live also." This refers to

His resurrection. When the Lord was resurrected, we were resurrected with Him. First Peter 1:3 tells us that Christ regenerated us in His resurrection. In His resurrection we were made alive together with Him. In this way we know that He is in us and we are in Him because He and we, we and He, have become one, and we live together. Therefore, to live after being born is to live with the Lord. The Lord lives and we also live; this is to live with the Lord.

John 20:22 says that after the Lord was resurrected and became the Spirit, He came into the midst of the disciples and breathed into them, saying, "Receive the Holy Spirit." The Lord Jesus passed through incarnation, death, and resurrection to become the breath of life. The Word is mentioned at the beginning of the Gospel of John: "In the beginning was the Word, and the Word was with God, and the Word was God" (1:1). Then the Word became flesh, and in the flesh He was the Lamb and the bronze serpent. After living thirty-three and a half years on the earth, He went to the cross as the Lamb to deal with our sins, our sinful deeds, and as the bronze serpent to deal with our sin, our sinful nature. Then He resurrected from the dead to become the life-giving Spirit. Thus, at the end of the Gospel of John, this Jesus Christ is the Spirit as the breath breathed into us for us to receive. Today this Spirit lives in us, that is, the Lord Jesus lives in us. In this way, not only were we regenerated, but we can also live because of the Lord. We have died to live—we have died with Him through baptism and live with Him in resurrection.

THE EVER-LIVING LORD LIVING IN US

In Revelation 1:18 John testified of Jesus Christ as the One who said that He is the living One, and He became dead but is living forever and ever. This is a word spoken to the churches. Today He is living in the heavens at the right hand of the throne of God, but this is not the point of emphasis. The importance of His being the living One is that He is living in us. He is living forever and is living in us. He told us that today He is still living. Therefore, He wants us to leave every kind of death and rise up to be the living church. This is the thought in Revelation 1, and it is the very point which I want to convey to you in this chapter. Praise the Lord, we can be regenerated because of Him, and after regeneration we can also live by Him!

Now we are clear that from eternity past, in the Lord was life. Then in time, the Lord became flesh, not only as the Lamb to solve the problem of our sins but also as the bronze serpent to solve the problem of our sin. Furthermore, He was resurrected from the dead to become the life-giving Spirit. Today if we open to Him from our innermost being to receive Him, He will come into us, and we will receive life and be regenerated. After this, He will be in us as our food to supply us that we may live and have life abundantly for us to live by Him.

How do you live by Him? First, you must realize that formerly you had only your life, but now it is no longer you but the Lord Jesus who is living within you. Therefore, today you are a dual person. Outwardly it is you, and inwardly it is the Lord Jesus; within you there are two lives. Second, God does not want you to live by your original life. God wants you to live by your second life, which is God Himself. Third, this second life is in your spirit. Thus, if you want to live by this life, you need to live by your spirit. Fourth, in your speech and action you should learn to slow down and not be in haste. You need to examine whether you are still living by your former life or are living by your second life. Are you speaking and doing things according to your emotions and moods or according to the spirit? Not only in big things but even in every small thing in your daily life, in every detail, you should carefully ask yourself, "Is this of my original life, or is this the Lord living within me? Am I speaking and doing things according to my emotions and moods or according to the Lord in me?"

EXERCISING TO LIVE BY THE LORD
FOR THE CHURCH LIFE

In this matter we must be diligent to have daily exercise. This is vastly different from self-cultivation or any religious doctrine. Rather, this is the living God, the living Lord, who is in us to be our life. In actuality, this is not a doctrine; rather, this is a spiritual, divine fact. This living Lord passed through incarnation, human living, crucifixion, and resurrection to become the life-giving Spirit. Today if you receive Him, you will be regenerated and He will live in your spirit. If you live by Him and not by yourself, you will be living Christ. This is being born to live, being regenerated to live Christ, to live Him out. This is the genuine Christian life, which is victorious and spiritual.

The issue of this living is the church. Therefore, for the church life we must all live in our spirit, exercising to live by the Lord.

CHAPTER TWO

LIVING WITH THE LORD

Scripture Reading: John 3:6b; 6:57b; 14:19; 1 Cor. 15:45b; 2 Cor. 3:17; 2 Tim. 4:22; 1 Cor. 6:17; Rom. 8:4; Gal. 2:20; Phil. 1:19-21a

In the previous chapter we briefly covered the matter of being born to live. After our regeneration we live because of the Lord. In this chapter we will go on to see the matter of living with the Lord.

THE CENTRAL REVELATION OF THE BIBLE

Living with the Lord is truly a mysterious matter. It is incredible that we human beings, especially sinners, can live with the Lord, who is divine and holy. This matter has been fully revealed and thoroughly explained in the Bible; moreover, it may be considered to be the center of the entire New Testament, and it is also a transparent truth. However, we do not have this concept when we come to read the Bible. On the contrary, we have many other concepts that are inaccurate, such as our natural concepts, our moral concepts, our religious concepts, and our cultural concepts. It is difficult for anyone to be freed from these four kinds of concepts. Our natural concept is that man should do good. Moreover, our religious concept is that man should do good to please God and to glorify God that he may worship God in peace. Regarding our cultural concepts, we know that whether people are from the East or from the West, they have their own culture and are very much influenced by their own culture. In addition, we have our moral concepts. People from every land are required to be moral and to keep moral standards in all human relationships. Thus, every one of us, young or old, has accumulated many old concepts. This is like wearing a pair of colored glasses; when we come to read the Bible, our natural, old concepts not only influence us but also veil us from seeing the true color, the center, and the fundamental revelations of the Bible. Instead, we see only the superficial things of the Bible.

In this chapter, we want to have an in-depth look at the Bible, and in particular we want to see the central matter in the New Testament. The central revelation in the Bible tells us that the Triune God—the Father, the Son, and the Spirit— has a move, a work, in two great steps. First, He accomplished redemption for us. We were sinners—corrupted, fallen people. As such, we deserved death and perdition, and we were utterly condemned and rejected by God. However, since God had chosen us, He could not abandon us. Therefore, the first step of His work was to accomplish redemption for us that He might rescue us, the fallen men, and solve the problem of our sins. He also justified and cleansed us completely that we might receive His redemption.

However, this is not the consummation; it is only the beginning. Therefore, God still has to carry out the second step of His work, that is, to work Himself into us. This is a mystery. God wants to work Himself into us; He does not want simply to give us something that is of Himself. He does not impart His life to us without coming into us Himself; rather, He works Himself into us to be our life. This life is God Himself. He comes into us to be our life, expecting that we will take Him as our life. We might think that God wants us to take Him as life and live by Him as life merely because He does not want our life, that He wants only His life because our life is bad, wicked, and corrupt. We cannot say that this thought is wrong, but it is not altogether accurate and it is not up to the standard. We must realize that even if our life were clean, sinless, and perfect, God still needs to and wants to come into us to be our life.

GOD'S GOAL AND WORK

When God created man, He created man in His image and after His likeness. Then man was completely like Him, not in the inward substance but in the outward appearance. This likeness in outward appearance refers not so much to the physical appearance but to the manifestation of virtues. God is love, so He created us with a loving heart; He is light, so He created us in such a way that we like to be in the light; He is holy, so He created us with a nature that dislikes to be associated with evil elements and desires to be transcendent and uncommon; and He is righteous, so He created us with a nature that demands justice and uprightness. God is love, light, holiness, and righteousness; therefore we, who were created by Him, are the same as He is in our psychology, nature, desire, and taste.

Everyone knows that it is right to love and wrong to hate. If you love someone, you will feel happy; if you hate someone, you will feel contempt. No one likes to do the things of darkness; everyone delights to do the things of light. Therefore, whenever we do anything of darkness, we try to hide ourselves, and whenever we do anything of light, we feel free to make a display. Although we may not know what holiness is, we all like to behave properly and not improperly. We all like to be transcendent and outstanding instead of being associated with evil elements. We also have an inner desire to be fair, just, and righteous. These are human virtues. These virtues are simply images that are without content. The content of these virtues is God. Our love is only an outward form; its content is God's love. We may use a glove as an illustration. A glove is made according to the form of a hand, but if the glove is not filled with the hand, it is empty. The glove by itself is empty; when you put your hand into the glove, the glove has its content, its inner reality.

When God created man, His intention was to put Himself into man. From the time He put Himself into us, we have had Him in us as our content. Now our love has reality, and our light has content; we are truly sanctified, and our conduct is fair, just, righteous, and upright. All these virtues are full of reality and content. Furthermore, this reality and content are altogether organic.

In the whole universe, God's plan, God's desire, God's eternal purpose, God's divine goal, is to work Himself into us.

However, before He could work Himself into man, man became fallen and corrupted; therefore, God had to redeem man. This redemption was not the goal but the procedure for Him to work Himself into man. Today, in their reading of the Bible for the study of the truths, many Christians stop at this step—God's redemption. They see only that we were fallen and corrupted, yet God became flesh to be our Savior by dying and shedding His precious blood for us on the cross. Therefore, we do not need to pay any price or do any work; to be saved we only need to repent and open ourselves to receive the salvation of the cross. We then are forgiven of our sins, cleansed from our defilement, and cleared of all charges against us. Consequently, the problems between us and God are solved; we are justified by God and reconciled to God. Now we are saved and will never go to hell, and one day we will go to heaven. This is the understanding of most Christians concerning God's salvation.

However, the Bible does speak not only about the first step of God's work, that God Himself became flesh to die for us. The Bible also tells us that God has a second step in His work. We have already seen that John chapter one says that in the beginning was the Word and the Word was God and that this God who was the Word in the beginning became flesh and tabernacled among us, full of grace and truth (reality). Then it says, "Behold, the Lamb of God" (v. 29). These things are believed and received by most Christians. Many preachers also speak and preach these things as their central message. They tell people that God so loved the world that He sent His beloved Son to become flesh and be a man, that this man was the Lamb of God who took away the sin of the world, and that if we confess that we are sinners and if we repent and receive this Savior, our sins will be forgiven, we will be reconciled to God, and we will even have fellowship with Him in peace. This is right, but it is not God's final goal; it is only the procedure for God to reach His goal. The goal of God is that after He has redeemed and cleansed us, He enters into us to be our life and become our nature and everything. The result is the union and mingling of God and man.

THE TWO "BECOMINGS" OF THE LORD JESUS

First Corinthians 15:45b tells us that the last Adam, who is the Lord Jesus, the incarnated Word, after passing through death and resurrection became a life-giving Spirit in resurrection. We know that the main subject of 1 Corinthians 15 is resurrection. Because some in the church in Corinth did not believe in resurrection, the apostle Paul corrected them and revealed to them the truth of resurrection. In this revelation Paul pointed out in particular that an important thing happened in resurrection: the last Adam, who became flesh and died for us on the cross, became a life-giving Spirit. In the context of 1 Corinthians 15:45 we see that Paul used an illustration when he referred to the matter of resurrection. He said that when a grain of wheat is sown into the earth, although apparently it dies, in actuality the life within does not die. The outward form of the grain dies and the shell decays, yet the life within grows. This growing is its resurrection. Once it is resurrected, it takes another shape, by which many grains are brought forth. This is the story of resurrection.

"This the secret nature hideth, / Harvest grows from buried grain" (*Hymns*, #482). No one can dispute this. The last Adam, the incarnated Jesus, lived on the earth for thirty-three and a half years, and then He died on the cross and was buried. People thought that He was finished. Little did they know that when they killed and buried the Lord Jesus, like a farmer who sows grain into the soil, they afforded Him the best opportunity to be resurrected. In this resurrection He took another form and became a life-giving Spirit.

It is a pity that today's Christianity neither sees this matter nor pays attention to the second half of 1 Corinthians 15:45. This is not an insignificant Scripture verse; it is as important as John 1:14. The Word became flesh, and the last Adam became a life-giving Spirit. The word *became* in these two verses is the same word in Greek. Moreover, this verb *became* in Greek denotes an action with a goal. This means that it is not a light move; it is an important action with a goal. Thus, the Lord Jesus took two important actions: first, He became flesh, and second, He became a life-giving Spirit.

He became flesh to be the Lamb for the redemption of sins. If He did not have flesh and blood, He could not make redemption for our sins. Therefore, John the Baptist said, "Behold, the Lamb of God" (John 1:29). This shows us clearly that the Lord became a man with blood, flesh, skin, and bones; therefore, He could die for us human beings, who also have blood, flesh, skin, and bones. The blood He shed was genuine human blood; in the eyes of God He is the Lamb. Therefore, Colossians 1:15 says that He is the Firstborn of all God's creation. Our Lord is the first of all the created things. If He were not created, He would not have flesh and blood; if He did not become a real man, a genuine man, He would not have blood and therefore could not have redeemed us.

The Lord Jesus was incarnated with blood and flesh. Hebrews 2 tells us that He Himself partook of blood and flesh, which were things created. In the time of the apostles, there was a group of people called the Docetists, who said that the Lord Jesus was not a real man and that His body was not a real body but a phantom. The name *Docetist* was derived from the Greek word meaning "to seem, to appear to be." John wrote 1 John 4 to refute this heresy. John said, "Every spirit which confesses that Jesus Christ has come in the flesh is of God, and every spirit which does not confess...is not of God; and this is the spirit of the antichrist" (vv. 2-3). Today there are some who call themselves fundamentalists yet say that the Lord Jesus is not a creature. If you say that the Lord Jesus is not a creature, you do not confess that the Lord Jesus has come in the flesh. Are you not then a Docetist? The Lord Jesus became a man, a creature; this does not mean that in becoming a creature He ceased to be the Creator. The fact is that He was God who became man and yet He was still God. He is God, thus He is the Creator; He became a man, thus He is a creature.

In the early 1960s when I was in Taipei, there was a so-called co-worker among us who did not believe that the Lord Jesus is still a man in the heavens today. Many Christians today also do not believe this. They believe that the

Lord Jesus was a man only when He was in the flesh, and He was a man until He died on the cross, but after His burial He ceased to be a man. Thus, in His resurrection He did not have the human nature and was no longer a man. The fact is that today the Lord Jesus is still a man. In 1 Timothy 2:5 the apostle Paul referred to Him as "the man Christ Jesus." Today He is the man, the Mediator of God and men. Not only so, after He was resurrected from the dead, He came to the midst of His disciples, appearing to them in His resurrected body for them to see and touch. This indicates that His resurrected body was a real entity and not a phantasm. He said to Thomas, "Bring your finger here and see My hands, and bring your hand and put it into My side" (John 20:27). Therefore, we can say that after His resurrection, the Lord Jesus was still a man with flesh and bones.

The first step the Lord Jesus took was to become flesh. As the Creator, He became a creature; this was God becoming man. As such a man, He was the Lamb of God who could shed pure and genuine human blood for the redemption of the human race. Then He took a second step, that is, He died and was resurrected, and in His resurrection He became the life-giving Spirit. In the first step, as God, He became a man—the last Adam; in the second step, the last Adam became a life-giving Spirit. The teachers of traditional theology say that the three of the Triune God—the Father, the Son, and the Spirit—are separated and independent of one another. Based on this they would dare not say that the Lord Jesus became the life-giving Spirit in resurrection and that this Spirit is the Holy Spirit, because if they say that this Spirit is the Holy Spirit, then the Father, the Son, and the Holy Spirit are not separated.

Actually, they do not need to be afraid or to preach in that way. They should not divide the Father, the Son, and the Holy Spirit in such a precise way. Revelation speaks of the Spirit of God as the seven Spirits, who are the seven eyes of the Lamb (Rev. 5:6). Traditional theologians cannot explain this. They say that the Son and the Holy Spirit are separated, but the Bible says that the Holy Spirit is the eyes of the Son; in other words, the Third of the Triune God is the eyes of the Second.

Not only so, in the evening of the day of resurrection the Lord Jesus came to His disciples. He breathed into them and said to them, "Receive the Holy Spirit" (John 20:22). This shows us that the Holy Spirit is the holy breath. The Holy Spirit received by the disciples was the breath breathed out by the Lord Jesus. Some may say that this was just a sign and not a reality, that the Lord Jesus did not really breathe into them for them to receive the Holy Spirit, that this was just a demonstration. Even if you could consider this matter of breathing into the disciples as a demonstration, there is no way to demonstrate the seven Spirits of God being the eyes of the Lord Jesus as the Lamb, as stated in Revelation.

THAT THE LORD IS THE SPIRIT
BEING THE PURE REVELATION OF THE BIBLE

Traditional theology of Christianity pays much attention to the Apostles' Creed, which was formulated in A.D. 325 under Constantine the Great. In that creed there was no mention at all of the seven Spirits. This shows that the Apostles' Creed was not complete. In history, at least three big groups of Christians officially declared that they want only the Bible and not the Apostles' Creed: the Brethren, the Southern Baptists, and the Church of Christ. I am afraid that some among us who are still under the influence of the old concepts may think that it is heretical to say that the Lord Jesus had genuine blood and genuine flesh, because it would then mean that He was a real man, a creature. For this reason, they cannot fully accept the statement that the Lord Jesus is the Firstborn of all creation. Regardless of whether people accept this fully, partially, or even not at all, I have to be honest and present to you the pure word of the Lord.

Furthermore, J. N. Darby's translation of the Bible is very clear about the Lord being the Spirit. Second Corinthians 3:6 says, "The Spirit gives life," and verse 17 says, "And the Lord is the Spirit." A note in J. N. Darby's translation indicates that verses 7 to 16 are a parenthesis; thus, verse 17 directly follows verse 6: "The Spirit gives life," and "the Lord is the Spirit." This linking of the Spirit with the Lord strengthens what is said in 1 Corinthians 15:45, that the Lord in His resurrection became the life-giving Spirit. Moreover, 2 Corinthians 3:17 shows us that these two—the Lord and the Spirit—are one, yet They are also two. Verse 17a says that "the Lord is the Spirit," whereas 17b says that "where the Spirit of the Lord is, there is freedom." The former says that the Lord is the Spirit, indicating that the Lord and the Spirit are one, while the latter says, "The Spirit of the Lord," indicating that the Lord and the Spirit are two. This is just like John 1:1, which says, "In the beginning was the Word, and the Word was with God." Therefore, the Word and God are two. Then the verse goes on to say, "The Word was God," so the two are one. Hence, we say that God is triune; He is three yet one. Otherwise, we would have three Gods. Today many Christians and Christian teachers subconsciously have three Gods in their thinking and hearts.

THE LORD BECOMING THE SPIRIT
TO ENTER INTO OUR SPIRIT AS LIFE

The Bible shows us that the Lord Jesus, who was God, took two big steps for the accomplishment of God's purpose. The first big step was that He was incarnated to be a real man with flesh and blood that He might be our Redeemer for the redemption of our sins. Then He took the second big step in His resurrection to become the life-giving Spirit. Today the Lord Jesus in whom we believe is not only the One who became flesh but also the One who died and resurrected. The Lord Jesus in whom we believe is the One who became flesh, who shed His blood for the redemption of sins, who died and was resurrected, and who dispenses life. When we believed into Him, first our sins were forgiven and we were redeemed, and second, He came into us. This is not only a doctrine; this is our experience. When you repent, confess your sins, pray, and believe in the Lord Jesus, you not only have peace within but have the forgiveness of sins so that the problems between you and God are resolved. After that you will feel that there is One who has come into you.

The Lord has surely come into you. However, if the Lord were not the Spirit, how could He come into you? Today there are some who say that the Lord is in heaven and not in us and that He is so great and man is too small to contain Him. Therefore, they say that the Lord is not in us, but rather that He has a representative, the Holy Spirit, who is representing Him within us. This is truly to twist the Bible. Nowhere in the Bible does it say that the Holy Spirit is the representative of the Lord Jesus. Rather, the Bible says that the Lord is the Spirit. Furthermore, throughout the centuries, many of the spiritual writings which are of value also clearly state that in the experiences of Christians Christ and the Holy Spirit are just one.

Now we have seen that the Lord Jesus was God. He became flesh for the accomplishment of redemption; He died and was resurrected for the dispensing of life that He might work Himself into us. Regardless of how wrong some theology is and how negligent some people are in reading the Bible, the fact is that everyone who repents, confesses his sins, and believes in the Lord Jesus by calling on His name, has the Lord Jesus in him. No one can deny this. This Lord Jesus is in us; there is not a representative, but rather He Himself is in us. The Lord Jesus is "He who descended out of heaven, the Son of Man, who is in heaven" (John 3:13). Not to mention after His death and resurrection, even when He was in the flesh, He was on earth as in heaven.

We must not consider the Lord Jesus with our small brain; we must consider Him only according to what the Bible says. On the one hand, Romans 8:34 clearly says that today the Lord Jesus is in heaven sitting at the right hand of God. On the other hand, verse 10 of the same chapter says that Christ is in us. These are two aspects of the Lord Jesus. We can use electricity as an illustration. There is electricity in this building, and there is also electricity in the electric power plant. They are not two electricities but one electricity. Our Lord, who is boundless, was resurrected from the dead and became the life-giving Spirit. Therefore, John 7:38-39 says that out of the innermost being of those who believe into Him will flow rivers of living water. This He said concerning the Spirit, whom those who believed into Him were about to receive, but the Spirit was not yet. At the time the Lord Jesus spoke this word, the life-giving Spirit was not yet, because the Lord had not yet been resurrected from the dead and had not yet been glorified. In other words, at the time He was resurrected from the dead and was thus glorified (Luke 24:26), He then was the life-giving Spirit. This is the biblical truth.

The Lord Jesus is not only our Redeemer but also our life-giving Spirit. Therefore, today by our believing in Him our sins have been forgiven, and we have been reconciled to God; at the same time, by our believing in Him He is in us. If the Lord were not the Spirit, how could we enter into Him? Because He is the Spirit, the life-giving Spirit, we entered into Him when we believed into Him. Therefore, 1 Corinthians 1:30 says that it is God who put us in Christ. By our believing into Him, we have entered into Him, the pneumatic Christ, and He has also entered into us.

Now this Redeemer has become the life-giving Spirit. When we believed into Him, God forgave us of our sins, and this life-giving Spirit entered into our spirit to regenerate our spirit. Therefore, John 3:6 says, "That which is born of the Spirit is spirit." To be regenerated in our spirit means that we have another life; the divine life entered into us in addition to the life which we have in our flesh. Thus, we were born twice and have two lives. The first time, we were born of the flesh of our parents, so we have the life of the flesh. The second time, we were born of the Spirit of God in our spirit, so we have the life of the Spirit. Our Lord, who is the life-giving Spirit, dwells in our spirit. Therefore, 2 Timothy 4:22 says, "The Lord be with your spirit." If our Lord Jesus were not the Spirit, how then could He be with our spirit? Obviously this is not an allegory but a factual statement, proving that today our Lord dwells in the spirit of those who have been saved. Furthermore, 1 Corinthians 6:17 says, "But he who is joined to the Lord is one spirit." If the Lord Jesus were not the Spirit and if we did not have a human spirit within, how then could we be one spirit with the Lord? Now we surely know that we have a human spirit within, and this spirit in us has been regenerated. Not only so, as the Spirit, the Lord Jesus has entered into our spirit to dwell in our spirit. Thus, the two spirits became one spirit. All these matters have been neglected in Christian theology.

LIVING AND WALKING
ACCORDING TO THE ONE MINGLED SPIRIT

The key to having a proper spiritual experience is realizing the fact that two spirits have become one spirit—the Spirit became one with our human spirit. Romans 8:4 says that we must walk according to the spirit. Authorities among Bible translators, particularly J. N. Darby, pointed out that it is difficult to say whether the word *spirit* in this verse denotes the Holy Spirit or our human spirit. In reality, it denotes the regenerated spirit indwelt by the Holy Spirit. Therefore, *spirit* in Romans 8:4 refers to the spirit that is two spirits becoming one spirit. It is also what we usually call the mingled spirit. Strictly speaking, we cannot find a verse in the New Testament that tells us to walk according to the Holy Spirit. Galatians 5:16 tells us to walk by the Spirit, who mingles with our spirit to become one spirit. Second Timothy 4:22 says, "The Lord be with your spirit." This spirit is also the spirit that is two spirits becoming one spirit. This is why 1 Corinthians 6:17 says, "But he who is joined to the Lord is one spirit." Therefore, it is basic for us Christians, the children of God, to walk according to this spirit, that is, the two spirits becoming one spirit.

Dear brothers and sisters, we all must live according to this spirit, the spirit that is two spirits becoming one spirit. When you live in this way, you are living with the Lord. In my youth I heard messages on living with the Lord, although at that time what I heard was mostly on walking with the Lord and not so much on living with the Lord. Noah walked with God, and Enoch also walked with God. At that time I really treasured this, and I kept searching for the way to walk with the Lord, but I could not get an answer. Then gradually I saw that today we are higher than Enoch; we do not co-walk but co-live. We live with the Lord. Co-walking is outward, whereas co-living is inward. This is what the Lord said, that in that day, the day of His resurrection, He would live, and we also would live (John 14:19). The Lord and we are two lives becoming one life and two spirits becoming one spirit. Two lives have become one life, and two spirits have become one spirit. The Lord Jesus said, "I am the vine; you are the branches" (John 15:5). The branches abide in the vine and the vine abides in the branches, and they bear fruit together. This is co-living. This is very mysterious and all too glorious!

LIVING WITH THE LORD TO LIVE CHRIST

The result of our living with the Lord is that we live out Christ, and thus Christ is always magnified in our body. It is not a matter of outward right or wrong; rather, it is a matter of our living Him in the spirit, in the one mingled spirit. This is what God wants today, and this is today's Christian life. The Christian life is neither religious nor moral; it is neither natural nor cultural. The Christian life is a life that is lived out of the two spirits becoming one spirit. When we speak, we speak out of this mingled spirit. When we do things, we do them out of this mingled spirit. Our going or not going to a certain place also comes out of this mingled spirit. This is to walk according to the spirit.

Although we do not stress morality, Paul said that when we walk according to the spirit, we spontaneously fulfill the righteous requirements of the law (Rom. 8:4). Although we do not pay much attention to so-called ethics, when we walk according to the spirit, our ethics will be the highest. The husband will love his wife even more, and the wife will subject herself to her husband even more. Because at this point, it is not we who are in subjection or we who love; rather, it is the Lord who lives out of us as our subjection and our love.

This is God's living in us, and this is also our living out God. These two spirits becoming one spirit is the greatest mystery in the universe; it is something incomprehensible to the human mind. However, we praise and thank the Lord that because God took these two great steps—becoming flesh in order to accomplish redemption for us and resurrecting from the dead in order to dispense Himself into us to be our life— we all have become Christians who have the mingled spirit and who live with the Lord. Hallelujah, we can live with Him!

CHAPTER THREE

MUTUAL ABIDING WITH THE LORD

Scripture Reading: John 15:4-5; 14:23; Rom. 8:9-10; 2 Tim. 4:22

GOD DESIRING TO ABIDE IN MAN TO BE MAN'S LIFE

The most mysterious matter in the Bible, something which we could never imagine or dream up, is that the Lord Jesus personally told His disciples that He wanted them to abide in Him and that He also wanted to abide in them. Since we have become accustomed to reading such a word, we are not amazed by it. However, if you were there on that day hearing this word, would you not have been astonished? You would wonder, "Is the Lord speaking something true? Is this an allegory, or is it only an illustration? What does this word really mean? How can we abide in the Lord? And how can the Lord abide in us? This is truly difficult to understand."

When the Lord Jesus spoke this word, He had already been living on earth for over thirty years. Formerly He had been a carpenter at home, but when He became thirty years of age He came out to speak for God to do the work of preaching. After doing this work for nearly three and a half years, one day He told the disciples that He would be leaving them. They had been with Him for three and a half years, and no one could help but love Him and be attracted to Him because He was such a marvelous, real, great, yet meek God-man. Every one of them liked Him. Therefore, in John 12, when the Lord came to the home of one of the disciples, the atmosphere of loving, appreciating, admiring, and adoring Him reached such a high peak that a sister poured ointment upon Him from her most treasured alabaster flask. The people's adoration for the Lord had reached the ultimate. He was very lovable. Moreover, His believers and followers anointed Him not only once. According to the record in the four Gospels, they anointed Him twice. In Luke 7 there was the other occasion when He was anointed. He was truly lovable and attractive.

Nevertheless, one day all of a sudden He told those who loved Him that He would be leaving them. When the disciples heard this, they became sorrowful. While they were in sorrow, He said to them, "Do not let your heart be troubled" (John 14:1, 27b). He also told them that He would go away and would come again (v. 28). Today there are Bible interpreters in Christianity who say that His going was His ascension, and His coming again will be His second coming at the end of the age. They say that the wait has been almost two thousand years, yet He has not come. However, this is not the meaning of the word the Lord Jesus spoke at that time. What He meant by His going was that He was going to the cross to die and that after His death He would be resurrected. His going was His death; His coming would be His resurrection. What the Lord meant by His word was: "Do not let your heart be troubled. My going is for your benefit, because if I do not go, I can only be among you. You love Me, and I also love you. However, my intention is not only to be among you but also to enter into you. I want to be not only among you as your gain, your enjoyment, and your Lord. More than this I want to enter into you to be your life. If I remain outside of you, I cannot be your life. For me to be your life, I must enter into you."

THOSE WHO EAT THE LORD LIVING BECAUSE OF HIM

If food does not enter into us, it has nothing to do with our life. For food to become our life, it must enter into us. Furthermore, it must not only enter into us but also become part of us. In this way the food that we eat becomes our life and life supply. Therefore, in John 6 the Lord Jesus said that He is our bread of life, that He who comes to Him shall by no means hunger, and that He who eats Him shall live because of Him (vv. 35, 57b). It is a pity that at that time the disciples did not understand the Lord's word because what He told them was new; this was a new utterance, a new concept. This word had never been uttered since the creation of the world. If someone today were to say that he is our food and that we must eat him, we would find this word hard to accept. We would definitely say that this man is crazy, that he is sick in his mind, and that he ought to be sent to the mental hospital. However, in John 6 the Lord repeatedly said that He is the bread of life. Those who eat Him shall live because of Him. Although the Lord said this repeatedly, not one of His disciples could receive His word. At the end of John 6, many of the disciples, after hearing this word, said, "This word is hard; who can hear it?" (v. 60). Then they went back and no longer walked with the Lord. Jesus said to the twelve, "Do you also want to go away?" Simon Peter answered Him, saying, "Lord, to whom shall we go? You have words of eternal life" (vv. 67-68). Although this was the reply at this time, they were all confused again in chapter fourteen.

In John 14, the Lord told the disciples that He was going, but He also said that after going He would come again. It was not that He would be gone for two thousand years and still not return. What the Lord meant in 14:19 was that in a little while He would return. The Lord went to die and to be buried. Shortly afterward He returned. Furthermore, the Lord assured His disciples that He would not leave them orphans and that after going He would come again. However, when the Lord came back, He would be another Comforter. He would come back as the Spirit of reality. John 14:16-20 describes this matter in a very clear way. The Lord Jesus was originally in the flesh and could be only among the disciples. Then this Lord in the flesh, who was the last Adam, went through death and resurrection and was transfigured to be the life-giving Spirit. This is just like a grain of wheat, after being put into the ground it grows into a different shape. Originally it was just a grain; but when it grows, it is a vibrant, lively, tender green sprout that is entirely different from its original shape. This tender green sprout continues to dispense life, gradually grows up to bring forth the stem, branches, and leaves, and eventually blossoms and bears fruit. This is altogether a matter of the dispensing of life.

People in Christianity today have not seen this matter clearly. They see the Lord Jesus only as the Almighty Lord, who could rise from the dead even though He was killed. Furthermore, after resurrection, He ascended into the heavens to be seated on the throne where no one could touch Him. This is the great Christ that they know. On the one hand, the Bible tells us that He truly is great—He is the King of kings and Lord of lords. On the other hand, however, the Bible tells us that Christ wants to be our life. The aspect of Christ being great can easily be seen. Everyone who reads the Bible can see it. However, the aspect of Christ being life is rarely seen. Almost everybody in Christianity is in darkness with respect to this matter of God being man's life; there is no one who speaks about this. I was born into Christianity, grew up in Christianity, was educated in Christianity, and was nurtured in Christianity. I do not know how many sermons I heard, yet I never heard the matter of Christ being man's life.

THE LAST ADAM BECOMING THE LIFE-GIVING SPIRIT

First Corinthians 15:45b says, "The last Adam became a life-giving Spirit." The Lord Jesus was God, the Word who was God from the beginning. This Word became flesh to be the last Adam. He was incarnated and had no blood and flesh to be our redeeming Lord. If He had not been incarnated, being without blood and flesh, He could not die for us and even more He could not shed His blood for us. Praise the Lord, He had flesh and blood so that He could die for us and shed real human blood to redeem us from sin! Praise the Lord, this is what the last Adam accomplished for us! Then He rested, and people buried Him in a new tomb hewn in the rock. After God finished the work of creation, He rested. Now again the Lord rested after accomplishing the work of redemption on the cross.

Not long after His death on the cross, the Lord resurrected. At the time He was raised from the dead, He was like a grain that had died in the earth and grown up in a different shape. This shape is a life shape, a life-giving shape. First

Corinthians 15, which is a chapter on resurrection, speaks of a grain being sown into the ground and growing into another shape. Then it speaks of the last Adam as such a grain resurrecting from the dead to become a "tender sprout," which is the life-giving Spirit. After a grain is sown into the earth, it dies and then grows up to be a tender sprout. This tender sprout supplies life so that the wheat can become fully grown and bear fruit a hundredfold.

The Lord said, "Unless the grain of wheat falls into the ground and dies, it abides alone, but if it dies, it bears much fruit" (John 12:24). We are the "much fruit," the many grains. He became the life-giving Spirit to impart life into us as the many grains. When we as the many grains are joined together, we become one bread, one Body, which is the church. Therefore, the issue of His death and resurrection as the one grain is the church. The church is produced by Christ in His becoming the life-giving Spirit. This life-giving Spirit is signified by the tender sprout. Once the tender sprout grows up, it begins to impart life. As a result, many grains are brought forth to become the Body of Christ, the church. If you see this light, you will then realize that the theology taught in Christianity concerning the Trinity is very shallow. Christian teachers speak about the Lord and the Holy Spirit as if the two were unrelated. However, if you see the light in 1 Corinthians 15, you will realize that Christ and the Spirit are related and that They are two yet one. When Christ was the last Adam, He walked, stayed, and lived with the disciples. After passing through death and resurrection, He became the life-giving Spirit. This life-giving Spirit is "the Spirit" in the New Testament. Before Christ's death and resurrection, the Spirit was not yet, as mentioned in John 7:39. However, after His death and resurrection, there was the Spirit. Today, the fact that we can be regenerated and become the many grains to be the Body of Christ is a result of the dispensing of life by the life-giving Spirit.

FIRST "IN" THEN "ABIDE"

In John 14 the Lord Jesus told the disciples not to be troubled by His going; rather, they should rejoice because in not more than seventy-two hours, He would come again. However, when the Lord came back He was no longer that seed. When He came again, He had become the tender sprout, which is the life-giving Spirit. When He came back, He entered into the disciples. At this time He was not only among them but was even in them. However, whether the Lord could spread in them, whether He could abide and expand in them, depended on whether they were willing to abide in the Lord. Therefore, in the next chapter He said, "Abide in Me and I in you" (15:4).

It is by our abiding in the Lord that we give the Lord the opportunity to spread Himself within us. When we abide in the Lord, the Lord abides in us. For example, if someone brings me to his house, when I go, I can only say that I am "in" his house. Whether I can remain there hinges totally on whether he welcomes me. If you invite me over for a meal, it will take two and a half hours at the most to finish the meal. Afterward you can rightfully say, "It is late; please go home to rest." Whether or not I stay depends on your attitude. Therefore, in John 14:23 the Lord said, "If anyone loves Me, he will keep My word, and My Father will love him, and We will come to him and make an abode with him."

In John 14, it is first "in" and then "abide." Verse 20 says, "In that day [that is, the day of the Lord's resurrection] you will know that I am in My Father, and you in Me, and I in you." Here the word is only "in" and not "abide." But in verse 23 there is the thought of abiding—to "make an abode." Today Christians often speak about the Lord being in them. They treasure His being in them. However, the Bible shows us that the Lord's being in them is the initial stage; first it is "in" and then "abide." First, He is in you, and then if you love Him, He will abide in you. The Lord has come, and He is in you to be with you. However, if you do not love Him, how can He abide in you? If you love Him and keep His word, then His Father and He will come to you to abide with you. Whether or not the Lord abides with you depends upon your attitude and response. You should have the response that you love Him and keep His word. The One you love is the Lord Jesus, and the words that you obey are His words, but it is amazing that

eventually the Father comes because of your love. Are They—
the Father and the Son—two or one? The Lord Jesus never
said that He and the Father are two. He said, "I and the
Father are one" (John 10:30). Here it does not say that the
Lord and the Father are united to be one. In the Gospel of
John we cannot see that the Lord and the Father are joined,
united, to be one. Rather, the Gospel of John shows us again
and again that the Lord and the Father are one.

John 14 shows us that first there is "in, and then there is
"abide." In chapter fifteen, the Lord Jesus explained this with
an illustration. He said, "I am the vine; you are the branches"
(v. 5). With respect to the life within, the branches are abiding
in the vine. The branches' abiding in the vine is the condition
for the vine's abiding in the branches. It is not that the vine
abides in the branches and then the branches can abide in the
vine. The vine's abiding in the branches is not the requirement for the branches' abiding in the vine. Rather, the
branches' abiding in the vine is the requirement for the vine's
abiding in the branches. After His death and resurrection, the
Lord became the life-giving Spirit, and in John 20 He came to
breathe into the disciples, saying, "Receive the Holy Spirit"
(v. 22). From that time on, the Lord was in them.

Today the Lord is truly in us. However, whether the Lord
can abide in us depends on our response. Do we love Him? Do
we cooperate with Him? Is it what He says that counts, or
what we say? If what we say counts, then it is finished. If
what He says counts, then it is wonderful. If we love Him and
keep His word, His Father will come with Him not only to be
in us but also to abide in us.

MUTUAL ABIDING WITH THE LORD

To be "in" is different from to "abide." In John 15 the Lord
said, "Abide in Me and I in you" (v. 4). This is a mutual abiding. However, most of us Christians understand this mutual
abiding as dwelling together. Husbands and wives dwell
together, but we are mutually abiding with the Lord. It is not
enough to dwell with the Lord; what God wants is mutual
abiding. This is something many Christians have not seen. In
our concept it is either walking with the Lord or being with

the Lord, while dwelling with the Lord is somewhat better, and living with the Lord is even better. What Christians have seen are walking with, being with, dwelling with, and living with. Our natural concept does not exceed "with." However, what the Bible tells us is not only walking with, being with, dwelling with, or living with, but even more it is mutually abiding in. If we walk with the Lord, we are with Him; if we are with Him, we dwell with Him; if we dwell with Him, we live with Him; and if we live with Him, we have the mutual abiding with Him. Our living with the Lord depends on our dwelling with Him; our dwelling with Him follows our being with Him, and our being with Him requires our walking with Him. In the Old Testament there is walking with God. In the New Testament we see there is *being* with the Lord. First, there is being with the Lord, then there is *dwelling* with the Lord. This dwelling with the Lord must reach the point of mutual abiding.

Mutual abiding means that we abide in the Lord and the Lord abides in us. The Lord Jesus wants to mutually abide with us. Without the mutual abiding, the Lord is not satisfied. How then can we abide in the Lord, and how can He abide in us? This is the most central and mysterious teaching in the Bible, yet it has been the most neglected by Christians. The Bible contains many words on the surface. We often illustrate this with chicken feathers and garlic husks. Chicken feathers are not good to eat, and garlic husks are undesirable. However, without feathers the chicken cannot survive, and without husks the garlic cannot grow. The garlic must have husks to grow properly, and for the chicken to grow well, it must have full feathers. When you buy a chicken, you must first examine the feathers. If the feathers are scraggly, do not buy the chicken because it will not be a good one. A chicken can be good only if it has good feathers; good feathers are a guarantee of a good chicken. Eventually, however, no one will eat the chicken feathers. If you invite me to eat chicken, you would not give me a plate of chicken feathers to eat. We northerners love to eat garlic, but you would not give me a pile of garlic husks to eat. That would be an insult to me.

Similarly, the vine spoken of in the Bible has a main stalk and supplementary branches and leaves.

Ephesians 5 says that we must be filled in spirit (v. 18), and not just filled but even overflowing with all the fullness of God. When we are filled unto all the fullness of God, what overflows may be a "chicken feather" such as wives submitting to their husbands, or it may be a layer of "garlic husks" such as husbands loving their wives. However, in reality it is the fullness of God that has filled us and has saturated our entire being so that we overflow God. As a result the wives spontaneously submit to their husbands, and the husbands spontaneously love their wives. How can garlic grow without a husk? However, Christianity has concentrated on details but forgotten the main objective. Instead of speaking about God's filling, their talk is about loving the wives and submitting to the husbands. This is the condition of many Christians today. They do not know the truth, nor do they know the reality of the Spirit; they teach people as religion the husks and feathers of the Bible.

The Lord's economy, which is entirely different from Christianity, is to dispense the Lord Himself into us not only to be our life but also to be our everything, thereby causing us to be filled with Him. After we are filled, what flows out from within us is God Himself. If you are a wife, then what flows out is submission to your husband. If you submit to your husband, it is not your virtue but the expression of God, the flowing out of God. If you are a husband, what flows out is love for your wife. Your love for your wife is not your characteristic but the overflow of God, the flowing out of God. What the wife overflows is submission; what the husband overflows is love. Whether submission or love, they are the overflow of God Himself.

MUTUAL ABIDING WITH THE LORD
BEING ALTOGETHER A MATTER IN THE SPIRIT

What is it to abide in the Lord? Our Lord was God, who became man to be the last Adam. Since Adam sinned, there was the need of another Adam to accomplish redemption. The first Adam sinned, but the last Adam came to redeem. Only the last Adam could redeem us because we are all descendants of Adam. The first Adam sinned causing all of us little Adams to fall into sin. Hence, the last Adam came to redeem us. However, there are those who do not wish to receive Jesus, but whoever is willing to receive Him will be redeemed. We thank and praise the Lord that here today we all are willing and we have received Him; thus, we have been saved. As our last Adam, He has redeemed us.

In this respect Christianity is right. However, Christianity is not willing to go on and see that this last Adam has now become the life-giving Spirit. He is not only the last Adam; even more He has become the life-giving Spirit. The last Adam is for redemption, whereas the life-giving Spirit is for dispensing life. His redemption on the cross is objective to us, but His dispensing of life must be subjective to us. Thus, as the life-giving Spirit He entered into us. Second Timothy 4:22 says, "The Lord be with your spirit." Today the Lord is in our spirit. Romans 8:9 says, "If indeed the Spirit of God dwells in you." Then it goes on to say, "Yet if anyone does not have the Spirit of Christ, he is not of Him." We have Christ; therefore, we belong to Christ and we are joined to Christ. Then verse 10 says, "But if Christ is in you." These few verses first mention the Spirit of God, then the Spirit of Christ, and then Christ. Never think that these three are three different ones. Rather, these three all refer to the same One. The Spirit of God is the Spirit of Christ, and the Spirit of Christ is Christ. After reading the entire context, you will see that today our God, our Savior Christ, is the consummated Spirit.

THE TRIUNE GOD PROCESSED AND CONSUMMATED TO BE THE ALL-INCLUSIVE, LIFE-GIVING SPIRIT

If the Lord Jesus did not go through death and resurrection, then there would not be the "story" of the life-giving Spirit. If He did not go through death and resurrection, there would only be the story of the last Adam. If God did not become flesh, there would not be the story of the last Adam; there would only be the story of God. God is in three stages: before His incarnation, He was the story of God; after He was incarnated to be a man, He was the story of the last Adam;

and after His death and resurrection, He became the story of
the Spirit.

However, it is sad that today Christianity receives Christ
only in certain aspects. One is the aspect of His being God
before He became flesh. Another is the aspect of His being the
last Adam in His becoming flesh to be a man. They also
receive Christ in the aspects of His being our Savior in His
death and resurrection, in His ascension to the heavens, and
in His being seated on the throne. However, Christ did not
stop there. Through death and resurrection He became the
life-giving Spirit. Today our Savior has been consummated to
be the Spirit. After His resurrection, He remains in resurrection and has entered into us. He is in resurrection and is
living in us. This is altogether a story of the Spirit. Today He
is the Spirit. This is not another Spirit that is apart from God.
God is Spirit and the Lord Jesus became the life-giving Spirit,
but this is not to say that the Spirit of God and the life-giving
Spirit are two different Spirits. The two Spirits are one Spirit.
Not only so, the Triune God has the aspect of being the
Father, the Son, and the Holy Spirit, but this is not to say that
God is Spirit and that the Holy Spirit is another Spirit.

God is Spirit, and from eternity He is Spirit. The title *the
Spirit of God* appears as early as Genesis 1:2. There it says
that the Spirit of God was brooding upon the surface of
the waters. According to essence, God is Spirit. However,
although God was Spirit before His incarnation, He had no
relationship with man and had no story of man. First of all,
one day God was born into Mary through the Holy Spirit.
After the conception was completed, He with the human
nature was born to be a God-man, possessing both divinity
and humanity. At that time the Bible began to use the title
the Holy Spirit for the Spirit of God. The title *the Holy Spirit*
was not used until the Lord Jesus was conceived to be born.
This title was not used in the Old Testament. The first record
of the Spirit of God is in Genesis 1; the first record of the Holy
Spirit is in Matthew 1. Matthew 1 shows us that this One
who was conceived in the womb of Mary and born of her was
of the Holy Spirit. He is sinless and holy; He is the Holy One.

From this time the Spirit of God began to have a relationship with man.

The Lord lived and worked on earth for thirty-three and a half years, and eventually He died on the cross to accomplish redemption. Then He was resurrected from the dead to become the life-giving Spirit. Before God was incarnated, He was Spirit. Even after He became flesh, He still could not be reckoned as the life-giving Spirit. For God to dispense life into man is not simple. He needed to go through many processes. As the divine Spirit He could not directly and suddenly come into man to give man life. There were still many problems in man, many problems that had not been solved. God had to first become man, pass through human living, and go to the cross to deal with all of man's problems, such as sin, the world, Satan, flesh, and the old creation. If these problems were not dealt with and terminated, then God could not dispense life into man. Suppose you want to put something into a vessel. If the vessel is dirty, you must first wash and even sterilize it; otherwise, the contents placed in the vessel would be contaminated. If God did not deal with all of our problems, He could not dispense Himself as life into us. Even though God is Spirit, without going through incarnation, death, and resurrection He would have no way of dispensing life into us. It was only through His incarnation, death, and resurrection that He could deal with all the problems. Hence, it was at the completion of all these processes that He became the life-giving Spirit. He is not merely the Spirit of God or the Holy Spirit but the life-giving Spirit. He advanced from being the Spirit of God to being the Holy Spirit, and then from being the Holy Spirit to being the life-giving Spirit. These are not three Spirits but one Spirit. By this time He had not only accomplished creation as the Spirit of God, He had not only accomplished redemption through the Holy Spirit, but even more He as the life-giving Spirit had consummated God's new creation, which is the church.

In this consummation, God is the life-giving Spirit. Today we are all in God's new creation, which is the church. This does not mean that we are not the created ones, nor does it mean that we have not been redeemed. Rather, it means that we have gone through creation and redemption and are now in the new creation, which is the church. What we need here is the life-giving Spirit. This life-giving Spirit is the Holy Spirit, and the Holy Spirit is the Spirit of God. Today this life-giving Spirit is the Triune God. Romans 8:10 says, "Christ is in you," and 2 Timothy 4:22 says, "The Lord be with your spirit." The Lord who is in us is the life-giving Spirit. This life-giving Spirit is the Triune God Himself, but this is not the God who had not gone through incarnation, death, and resurrection. Because He has gone through incarnation, death, and resurrection, He is now in us as the One who has been processed. In Genesis 1, He had not gone through the process, but today in the Epistles in the New Testament, He is a processed God. He is the Triune God who has passed through incarnation, death, and resurrection. Today He is the life-giving Spirit dwelling in our spirit.

MUTUAL ABIDING WITH THE LORD— WE ABIDING IN THE LORD AND THE LORD ALSO ABIDING IN US

The Triune God was incarnated, passed through human living, died on the cross to accomplish redemption, and entered into resurrection to become the life-giving Spirit. Today He enters into us to abide in our spirit with all that He has, all that He has gone through, all that He has accomplished, and all that He is. We must remember that He abides in us and that He very much desires that we abide in Him. Therefore, every day from morning to evening, in big things or in small things, in our home or outside our home, and in all our living and actions we must abide in Him. When we want to speak to others, unless we have the assurance that we are abiding in Him, we should not speak. We speak only when we have the assurance that we are abiding in Him. We speak from within Him, not outside of Him. Before we argue with others, we must examine to see if we are abiding in the Lord. We must first abide in the Lord and then argue. The Lord is already abiding in us; so before we do anything, we must first abide in the Lord. We act after we are abiding securely. It is easy to speak about abiding in the Lord, but it is not easy to live this out. Therefore, we must learn to practice abiding in the Lord in our daily life.

The secret to abiding in the Lord is first to see that our Lord was God and therefore had the stories of God. Then He became flesh to be the last Adam and thereby had the stories of the last Adam. After this, He accomplished redemption through death and resurrection to become the life-giving Spirit, so He has the stories of the life-giving Spirit. Today He is abiding in our spirit. At this time, He abides in us not only as God but also as man, as One who passed through all the experiences of human living and who died and resurrected. Not only so, He is also the Spirit. In this Spirit, there are the element of man, the element of God, and the elements of incarnation, human living, death, and resurrection. Now He wants us also to abide in Him. Before we do anything in our daily living and walk, we must first abide in Him. We abide and then live; we abide and then walk. All our living and our walk must be expressed in this abiding, in which all our problems are gone. In this abiding, He as the indwelling, all-inclusive Spirit solves all our problems, eliminates our preferences, and kills our lusts.

Prior to 1958 I preached very much about the cross and also about resurrection. Then in 1958 I saw further that although there is nothing wrong with preaching the cross, without the Spirit it is vain. Resurrection also is real, but without the Spirit, even the preaching of resurrection is vain. I am not saying that we do not want the preaching of the cross or that we do not want the cross; nor am I saying that we do not want the preaching of resurrection or that we do not want resurrection. Rather, I am saying that it is useless to preach the empty word of the cross. Many people know the word of the cross yet live a defeated life. They even lie and do harm to others. Where is the cross? Where is resurrection? Dear brothers and sisters, what we need is this all-inclusive Spirit, the One who has gone through death and resurrection to become the life-giving Spirit. In Him is God; in Him is our Savior; in Him is the killing effect of the cross; and, even more, in Him is the power of resurrection.

Hence, we must abide in this Spirit. This Spirit today is

in your spirit, and in Him there are different elements, including the killing effect of the cross and the power of resurrection. Thus, when you abide in Him, He kills your natural being, your flesh, your lusts, and your desires. As an illustration, your hands are covered with germs, but you may have a bottle of antiseptic solution. If you put your hands in the solution and allow them to abide there for five minutes, your hands will be clean. The preaching of disinfectants cannot kill the germs, nor can you shake off the germs from your hands. Only one thing will work, which is to let your hands abide for a while in the antiseptic solution. Before you do anything, you must abide for a while in your spirit. After you abide there for half a minute, all the "poison" will be killed.

If you are not in the Spirit, the word of the cross and of resurrection will be useless. It is this all-inclusive Spirit that contains the all-killing effect of the cross. It is this powerful Spirit that contains the power of resurrection. You must abide in Him for a while. If you abide for half an hour, you will be soaked with the Lord. If you abide for half an hour and then go to reason with others, your reasoning will be gone. The power of the Lord's resurrection and also the effect of His death will have killed your natural reasoning. Having been saturated with the power of resurrection, you will have the ability to humble yourself and apologize to others instead. This is the Lord's salvation. This is what Philippians 1:19 says: "This will turn out to salvation through...the bountiful supply of the Spirit of Jesus Christ." This is the bountiful supply of God as the all-inclusive Spirit, the Spirit of Jesus Christ. When you abide in Him, you are soaked with Him. When you abide in Him, you give Him the condition to abide in you. Thus, you will enjoy all His riches.

In summary, first, you must know that today your Savior is this Spirit abiding in you. Second, before you do anything in your daily living and walk, you must abide in Him. The Lord said that He will abide in the one who abides in Him. If you abide in Him, you will enjoy His salvation and all of His riches.

Chapter Four

WALKING ACCORDING TO THE SPIRIT

Scripture Reading: 1 Cor. 15:45b; 2 Cor. 3:17-18; 1 Cor. 6:17; 2 Tim. 4:22; Rom. 8:16, 4

THE WONDERFUL REVELATION IN THE BIBLE

In the previous three chapters we saw the matter of our living with the Lord and our mutual abiding with the Lord. In this chapter, we want to see the matter of walking according to the spirit. Apparently, this chapter is unrelated to the previous chapters, but in actuality it is the issue of the previous chapters. The Bible is the most wonderful book, in which the most wonderful matter is that the Spirit of God is mingled with our human spirit and that we should live and walk according to such a mingled spirit.

Among the Chinese people *The Great Learning* and *The Doctrine of the Golden Mean,* two of the Confucian *Four Books* in the Chinese classics, may be considered the highest books. *The Great Learning* says that the doctrine of great learning lies in developing the bright virtue, whereas the teaching of the Bible lies in the spirit and in walking according to the spirit. The phrase *develop the bright virtue* seems very profound in wording, but actually there is nothing mysterious in it. While the phrase *walk according to the Spirit* is simple in wording, the mystery within cannot be exhausted. The Bible is wonderful in that, first, it reveals a wonderful person and, second, a wonderful salvation. Although this wonderful person in the Bible has passed through two thousand years of human research, He remains mysterious and unfathomable. Isaiah 9:6 says that the name of this wonderful person is called "Wonderful Counselor." This wonderful One, Jesus, is wonderful not only in the Bible but also in the six thousand years of human history. Not only is His person wonderful, but His deeds, His might, and His transcendence are also difficult for us to comprehend.

THE WONDERFUL PERSON OF THE LORD JESUS

Napoleon occupied a dominant position for a period in history, but eventually he was banished to an island for imprisonment. Before he died, he confessed that Jesus was the Lord of heaven and of earth. Even the atheistic communist countries use the calendar of Jesus Christ. According to Chinese history, whoever was in power, his calendar would be used. Thus, the communist countries also admit today that the whole earth is under the ruling of Jesus. Jesus Christ is so wonderful that He is unsearchable and unspeakable.

Another wonderful thing in the Bible is the matter of the Triune God. In these past two thousand years, among theologians, Bible scholars, and Bible-studying preachers, there have been many debates concerning the Trinity—the Holy Father, the Holy Son, and the Holy Spirit. Is Jesus Christ the Father or the Son? Of course, most Christians would say that He is the Son, not the Father. However, the Bible says that Jesus Christ is the Son and also the Father. In John 14:9, the Lord Jesus said, "He who has seen Me has seen the Father." Some say that to see the Son is to see the Father because the Son represents the Father, but this does not prove that the Son is the Father. However, in verse 10 the Lord Jesus went on to say, "I am in the Father and the Father is in Me." This cannot be explained simply by saying that the Son represents the Father.

John 1:1 says, "In the beginning was the Word, and the Word was with God, and the Word was God." This statement involves a great deal. John initially said that the Word was with God; therefore, They must be two. But John also said that the Word was God, indicating that the two are one. Then, are God and the Word one or two? To this day, no one can fully explain this. In reality, He was the Word, and He was also God. Then John said that the Word became flesh and tabernacled among us (v. 14). Furthermore, he said, "Behold, the

Lamb of God" (v. 29). He was the Word, God, the flesh, the tabernacle, and the Lamb. Doctrinally speaking, since He was God, how could He be the Lamb? Not only so, He was the complete God, not the partial God. In the beginning was the Word, and the Word was God. This Word was the Lord Jesus; hence, the Lord Jesus was God, even the complete God—the Father, the Son, and the Holy Spirit.

Some may ask, since God is the Father, the Son, and the Spirit, and since the Lord Jesus is the Son, then is the Lord Jesus only one-third of the Triune God, being neither the Father nor the Spirit but only the Son? However, in his Gospel, John clearly stated at the outset that the Word was God, and this God was the complete God—the Father, the Son, and the Spirit. Hence, the statement "the Word was God" refers not only to the Father, only to the Son, or only to the Spirit, but to the entire God, that is, the Father and the Son and the Spirit. Since the Word was God, this Word must be the Father, the Son, and the Spirit as the complete Triune God. We cannot say that the Lord Jesus as the Word was only the Son but not the Spirit or the Father; otherwise, we would contradict the truth in the Bible. This is why Isaiah 9:6 says that a son is given to us and His name is called the Eternal Father. Second Corinthians 3:17 says, "The Lord is the Spirit." Furthermore, 1 Corinthians 15:45b says, "The last Adam became a life-giving Spirit." All these verses show us that the Lord Jesus is too wonderful. We cannot use our limited mind to restrict Him. He is all in all.

Colossians 1:15 tells us that Christ is the Firstborn of all creation. Some may argue that since Christ is the Creator, He cannot be a creature. But both the Bible and history tell us that this Creator at one time became a man with bones, blood, and flesh. Having a body of blood and flesh proves He was created. He is not only the Creator but also a creature. It is illogical to say that a man is not a creature. The Lord Jesus is a genuine man with genuine human blood. His blood is not the blood of goats and calves which cannot obtain redemption for man's sins. The blood of goats and calves cannot accomplish redemption for man's sins because it is only a type and a shadow. In the first and second centuries, there was a group of people called the Docetists, who said that since Jesus Christ is holy, He could never have had the defilement of human flesh. They also said that His body was not real flesh and blood but was merely a deceptive, transient phantom, and therefore He did not suffer, die, and resurrect. Such a great heresy was condemned by the apostle John in his first Epistle (4:1-3 and note 1 of verse 3).

The Bible tells us not only that the Lord Jesus was a man when He was on the earth but also that He was still a man even after His resurrection. In the evening of the day of His resurrection, He showed His body to the doubting disciples because they thought He was an apparition. The Lord Jesus told them that He had bones and that they could put their finger into His side to touch the wounds. To this day, our Lord Jesus is still a man in the heavens. When Stephen was stoned to death, he lifted up his eyes and said, "Behold, I see the heavens opened up and the Son of Man standing at the right hand of God" (Acts 7:56). This One spoken of in the Bible is so wonderful; therefore, we must not limit Him or visualize Him according to our imagination. We should speak according to the Bible and believe what the Bible says. We should speak, believe, and receive whatever the Bible says.

THE WONDERFUL SALVATION OF THE LORD

In Taipei more than twenty years ago I spoke on what Christ is. I had discovered nearly three hundred items from both the Old and New Testaments concerning what Christ is. He is truly too wonderful; He is the wonder of all wonders. Actually, He is everything; He is the Lord, God, the Triune God, the Holy Father, the Holy Son, and the Holy Spirit. If there is God in the universe, then He is God. If there is man in the universe, then He is the most distinguished man and the real man. If there is a Savior in the universe, He is also the Savior. If God needs sacrifices and lambs, then He is the sacrifices and the Lamb. He is all in all. Since He is so wonderful, the salvation which He accomplished is also wonderful.

Unfortunately, most Christians understand the salvation of Jesus Christ according to their human concepts. They think that we need a Savior firstly because of our sins and secondly because of our afflictions and woes. Therefore, we need a merciful Savior to deliver us from our sins and our afflictions. In China, not many believe in the Lord Jesus solely because of sins, but a great number believe because of sufferings. The Chinese people have the Buddhist concept of great mercy and compassion. Thus, the new believers of the Lord Jesus usually have the thought of Jesus having great mercy and compassion, though they may not say it. In the past I prayed with some after they first heard the gospel. When they opened their mouth, they often said, "O Savior of great mercy and compassion." Gradually, they stopped praying in this way because they observed that we did not pray like this. According to the human concept, we always think that we need a Savior because we are so wicked, sinful, and full of sufferings.

THE TWO ASPECTS OF THE LORD'S SALVATION

In actuality, the Lord's salvation is of two aspects. The first aspect is mainly for solving the problem of our sins. Through His crucifixion the Lord Jesus solved this problem. Since God is righteous, sin became a problem before Him. As our Redeemer, the Lord Jesus died on the cross and solved the problem of sin. The Bible shows us that on the cross the Lord Jesus as the Lamb became our sin offering and our trespass offering to deal with our double sin—our sinful nature within and sinful deeds without. On the cross He was judged by God on our behalf and shed His precious blood; hence, God could forgive us. His precious blood not only cleanses us of our sins, but it is also eternally efficacious.

There is another aspect of salvation which is much deeper than the first aspect and is related not only to what the Lord Jesus accomplished for us on the cross. Based on the redemption accomplished on the cross, He has entered into us to be our life, our nature, and even all the elements of our entire inward being, so that we can live not by ourselves but by Him. Some may understand that our living by Him means that we have to live outwardly in a manner which is proper, good, bright, holy, and overcoming. This understanding is superficial and incomplete. The main intention of the Lord Jesus' living in us is to transform us.

I often like to use tea as an illustration. The Chinese make tea by adding water to tea leaves. When the tea leaves are immersed in the water, the water is transformed. Originally, it was a cup of plain water, but when you put tea leaves into it and cover it, after five minutes the plain water is completely transformed. The nature, color, and flavor of the tea leaves enter into the water and transform it into tea. Water becomes tea because the element of tea has entered into the water. Christ is the tea, and we are the water. When the element of tea gets into the water, the water becomes tea. Likewise, when Christ enters into us, we become Christians. Hence, "Christian" means "Christ-man." We all are Christ-men because Christ has entered into us, and He is transforming us with His element. This is too mysterious.

Confucius spoke of developing the "bright virtue," which is to develop and magnify the bright virtue that we had originally. However, the Lord's salvation is not to develop and magnify what we had originally. Rather, He Himself comes into us to be our essence and element. This is truly a mystery. Originally, there is no other element in the water, but after the tea leaves are placed into the water, the element of tea is added into the water. Thus the water becomes tea. Originally, we did not have Christ in us, but now Christ has entered into us. The entrance of Christ into us adds a new element to us. Christ as the new element is God, the Lord, life, holiness, righteousness, and light. He is all in all. He is the Son with the Father. Moreover, in reality, the Son is the Spirit. Therefore, He is the Father, the Son, and the Spirit. He is all in all.

THE MYSTERY OF GOD BECOMING FLESH

Not only so, the Bible speaks first of Christ being God and then of Christ becoming man. God becoming man is truly a mystery. In the universe, there is such a One who lived on the earth two thousand years ago for thirty-three and a half years. Today, as you read the Gospels in the New Testament, you may not sense that these records are very marvelous. But if you would quietly consider that one day the Creator of the heavens and the earth actually became a man and grew up in the despised city of Nazareth in the home of a poor and lowly carpenter, you would realize how wonderful this is! The Creator of all things did not come to the earth for a short visit, as He did with Abraham in Genesis 18. Instead, He lived on the earth for thirty-three and a half years.

In Genesis 18, when Abraham was cooling himself at the tent door, three men came, two of whom were angels and the third was Jehovah God. Most people know only that Jesus became flesh to be a man two thousand years ago. But in reality, He came to visit Abraham in the likeness of a man four thousand years ago, even before He became flesh. Abraham washed His feet and served Him a meal with fine flour and a calf. The Southern Baptists published an article about their faith, quoting many Scripture verses as the basis of their faith. Concerning Christ, one of the verses quoted is Genesis 18:1. They said that the Jehovah in Genesis 18:1 was Jesus Christ. Some may question, "How could He have the form of a man at that time, and not only so, even have the reality of a man?" He was there, and Abraham washed His feet; He even ate the meal which Abraham's wife Sarah prepared for Him. The Bible is truly mysterious, and God is likewise mysterious. Even the theologians cannot explain these things.

THE LAST ADAM BECOMING THE LIFE-GIVING SPIRIT

We can only receive the spiritual and mysterious things according to the plain words of the Bible. The Bible states plainly that He was God who became a man. Then, at the fullness of thirty-three and a half years, according to the day, month, and year prophesied in the Scriptures, that is, on the fourteenth day of the first month when the lamb of the Passover was slain, the Lord Jesus was killed on the cross. When He was crucified, He was truly the passover Lamb who died for us to deal with our sins. He was buried and was resurrected on the third day, and at the time He was resurrected, He became the life-giving Spirit. First, He was God who became a man, that is, the last Adam. He passed through thirty-three and a half years of human living and eventually died on the cross. After passing through death and resurrection, the last Adam became a life-giving Spirit. The first step was that God became a man, and the second step was that this man became a Spirit. On the evening of the day of His resurrection He came into the midst of His disciples as a spirit, yet with bones and flesh. This is truly beyond our understanding. Not only is God a mystery, even we ourselves are a mystery which we cannot comprehend.

On the one hand, the Bible tells us that the Lord Jesus was God who became a man as our Savior to bear our sins on the cross. On the other hand, the Bible tells us that He died and resurrected, and in His resurrection He became the life-giving Spirit to enter into us. Now that we have Him in us, we can have an unveiled face before Him. Second Corinthians 3:18 says that we are like mirrors continually beholding and reflecting the Lord. Not only so, this reflecting causes us to be transformed into His image, even as from the Lord Spirit. This Lord is now the Spirit, who is in us transforming us into His glorious image. First Corinthians 6:17 says, "But he who is joined to the Lord is one spirit." We are one spirit with the Lord in our spirit, not in our mind, emotion, and will. Thus, Paul said to Timothy, "The Lord be with your spirit" (2 Tim. 4:22). This may be a simple statement, yet it is a great blessing. This statement implies two important points. First, the Lord must be Spirit. If the Lord were not Spirit, how could He be in our spirit, and how could He be with us? Second, we also must have a spirit in us. It is in our spirit that the Lord is with us. Romans 8:16 says, "The Spirit Himself witnesses with our spirit that we are children of God." There are two spirits within us: one is our spirit and the other is the Spirit, the Lord Jesus Christ.

WALKING NOT ACCORDING TO THE FLESH BUT ACCORDING TO THE SPIRIT

Dear brothers and sisters, I believe that you all are now clear. Today, our Lord Jesus, who was God, became a man who died on the cross to be our Savior to deal with our sins. Furthermore, He was resurrected from the dead and became the life-giving Spirit to dwell in us and be mingled with our regenerated spirit. Hence, there are not two spirits in us because actually these two spirits have been mingled into one spirit, just as tea and water are mingled into one. If you want to drink tea, you do not drink water first and then tea. When you drink, you get both the tea and the water because they have been mingled into one. Now the Lord as the Spirit has been joined and mingled with our spirit into one spirit. Thus, Romans 8:4 says, "That the righteous requirement of the law might be fulfilled in us, who do not walk according to the flesh but according to the spirit." We are those who walk according to the spirit. In Greek, there is no definite article before *spirit;* hence, it is difficult for the Bible translators to determine whether the spirit here refers to the Spirit or to our spirit. Why? This is because the two have become one—the two spirits have become one spirit. Just as in making tea, it is difficult to say whether it is tea or water in the cup.

The Greek word for *walk* in the phrase *walk...according to the spirit* denotes our living, our moving, our conduct, our actions, and our existence. The Bible teaches us and tells us that all those who are saved know that there is God in the universe. This God became a man to die for our sins and was resurrected to be the Spirit to dwell in our spirit. Now what He requires of us is that in our living, our walk, our conduct, and our every word and action we have our being according to the mingled spirit within. If you remember this and practice it, you will be truly blessed. To walk according to the spirit is not to walk according to human effort. Whenever you walk according to the spirit, the Spirit comes out and the Lord Jesus is lived out because He is in your spirit. Hence, we should all practice to live according to the spirit. Walking according to the spirit should be the motto of our living. How good it is to do everything, whether big or small, according to the spirit!

CHAPTER FIVE

EXERCISING TO BE ONE SPIRIT WITH THE LORD

Scripture Reading: 1 Cor. 6:17; 2 Cor. 3:17; 2 Tim. 1:7; 4:22

THE CENTRAL THOUGHT OF THE BIBLE

In this message we will consider the matter of exercising to be one spirit with the Lord. This sentence, recorded in 1 Corinthians 6:17, is the most mysterious sentence in the Bible. We believers in the Lord can actually become one spirit with the Lord. This is the most central teaching in the Bible. It is true that there are many moral and ethical teachings in the Bible. I believe that if we were to take everything written by the Chinese philosophical, classical scholars concerning ethics and morality and put them together with all the teachings and writings of Confucius and Mencius, they still would not say as much as the Bible does, and their standard would be much lower than the Bible's. For the human race, the Bible teaches the most about ethics and morality and has the highest standard. However, these teachings are not the center but the periphery of the Bible; they are the "branches" and not the "roots and trunk" of the Bible.

The center, the "roots and trunk," of the Bible is that we saved ones have become one spirit with the Lord. This declares two facts. First, the Lord must be Spirit. If He were not Spirit, how could He become one spirit with us? Second, even though we are not spirit, we must have a spirit; otherwise, how could we become one spirit with Him? According to our inward reality, we certainly have a spirit. When God created us, He made a spirit for us. Zechariah 12:1 says, "Jehovah, who stretches forth the heavens and lays the foundations of the earth and forms the spirit of man within him."

Our spirit within us was created by God, and according to
this verse, our human spirit is as important as the heavens
and the earth. This verse mentions only three things: the
heavens, the earth, and the spirit of man; it does not mention
any other item. Thus, the heavens, the earth, and the spirit of
man are of equal importance. Our human spirit is as important as the heavens and the earth; this is a tremendous
matter. If you understand the Bible and you know the meaning of the existence of the universe, you will see that the
heavens are for the earth, the earth is for man, man's center
is his spirit, and man's spirit is for containing God. Man is a
vessel for God to enter into and dwell in. This is the central
matter in the Bible.

THE MYSTERY OF THE HUMAN SPIRIT

I believe that the ancient Chinese sages had true wisdom
given to them by God. Some of their words have never been
duplicated by philosophers from other places. For example,
they said that man is the spirit of all creation. It is very
meaningful that the ancient Chinese sages used the word
spirit. Instead of saying that man is the head of all creation,
they said that man is the spirit of all creation. Moreover,
despite the fact that the Chinese classical scholars did not
have the clear revelation of the Bible, they studied the inward
human condition according to the science in their classics and
discovered the fact, which was spoken by Wang Yang-ming,
that within man there is an innate knowledge of good and an
innate ability to do good. They also discovered that such an
innate knowledge and ability is our conscience within us. In
his book called *The Great Learning,* Confucius spoke of the
way of great learning, which was very difficult for the classical scholars to explain: "The way of great learning is to
develop the bright virtue." In the term *bright virtue, bright* is
an adjective and *virtue* is a noun. The meaning of bright
virtue is a bright and shining moral virtue. The Chinese philosophers developed this point very much; the emphasis of
their moral and ethical teachings was to brighten the bright
virtue, which means to develop and increase the function of

the conscience, that is, man's innate knowledge of good and ability to do good.

We can see that whether people are civilized or barbarian, Chinese or from abroad, all have something within them. You may call it the conscience, the innate knowledge and ability, or the bright virtue, but within you there truly is such a thing. Many times there are lusts within you. For example, if you see that your classmate in school has a very good pen, you may think of a way to steal it. When you do this, you are outside of your spirit; you are in the improper functioning of your lusts, emotions, and mind. But on the other hand, while you are doing this, you sense an inner voice condemning you, even forbidding and criticizing you. Sometimes after you have stolen something, you feel uneasy using it. This feeling of uneasiness is not from any outward religious or ethical teaching. According to their studies of all the aspects of the conditions manifested in the human body and heart, Confucius and Mencius reached a conclusion that there was truly such a thing within man, and they called that thing the conscience. Later, Wang Yang-ming studied it further and called it the innate knowledge of good and the innate ability to do good. It is not only a knowledge but also an ability—a knowledge of good and an ability to do good. Knowing good and being able to do good are the functions of the conscience. If we add together the conscience, the knowledge of good, and the ability to do good, they equal the bright virtue.

You may not have stolen anything, but sometimes you argue with your mother. Daughters especially like to argue with their mothers. Your mother loves you, and you love her, but you still like to argue with her. Even before you finish arguing, while you are still quarreling, something inside tells you not to argue. Outwardly you are arguing, but inwardly you feel bad. There is a forbidding within which is the functioning of the conscience.

The Bible shows us that the conscience is the principal part of our spirit. When we preach the gospel, we mainly want to move people's conscience. When the conscience is moved, the spirit is moved. A real repentance comes from the conscience being touched. When the conscience is touched, the spirit is moved, and when the spirit is moved, the person's mind turns. In Greek the meaning of *repent* is a turning of the mind. A person's mind turns because his spirit is touched. Therefore, when we preach the gospel, it is not enough to speak mere doctrines. To speak doctrines is to try to convince a person's mind by reasoning. This does not work. We need the power of the Holy Spirit to touch and move people's conscience. Whenever a person's conscience is moved, his spirit is moved.

Once there was a preacher in China named John Sung. He went to America to study and received three Ph.D.s. When he preached the gospel, his messages were not up to the standard of the truth, but he had the power to touch people. When he spoke of salvation, he spoke not only with his mouth; he wore the traditional Chinese costume, and under his long gown he had bag after bag of props. Sometimes while he was speaking, he would pull out a small wine bottle and act out a person getting drunk and beating his wife. Later, he would take out some playing cards and act out a person gambling and shouting. Then he would take out an opium pipe and act out a person smoking opium. At the end of his preaching, he would reach into his pocket and pull out a small coffin. He said that the drunkard, the gambler, and the opium addict would all wind up in the coffin. When people listened to him speak, they did not have the slightest feeling that they were listening to a sermon, but their conscience could not help but be touched by him. When he finished speaking, great crowds of people would leave their seats, shedding tears as they walked to the front, weeping, praying, and repenting.

My elder sister once heard him preach the gospel in Honan Province. One time while John Sung was preaching, he pulled out a small pointer. As he was speaking, he pointed it at a woman and said, "You are someone's concubine." That woman was furious. She said to herself, "How could Christians be so unreasonable? They compelled me to come to their chapel to listen to the preaching and then revealed my status to the preacher." She had this reaction because she really was a concubine. She hated the person who brought her there, and she also hated the preacher. However, when she returned home and thought things over, the Holy Spirit worked in her and said to her, "How can you hate them? Are you not a concubine? You see, you are a sinner. If you were a proper person, how could you be someone's concubine?" This woman repented and went to listen to the preaching again on the following day. It was not the speaking of doctrines that convinced her reasoning and persuaded her to admit that she should not be a concubine. It was the power of the Holy Spirit touching her conscience. When her conscience was moved, her spirit was moved, and her mind was turned. This is repentance.

THE HIGHEST CHRISTIAN LIFE

Today we must see that the central teaching of the Chinese sages was to promote and develop the innate knowledge of good and the innate ability to do good. This innate knowledge and ability is our conscience, which is a part of our spirit. However, the Bible does not merely speak of the function of our conscience, which causes us to repent and confess our sins. The Bible also tells us that as soon as we repent and believe in the Lord Jesus, His redeeming blood cleanses us from our sins and His Spirit enters our spirit. The Lord in whom we believe is the God who created the universe; He is the real and living One. This God who is Spirit has actually entered into us. However, before He could enter us, He first had to be incarnated as a man, go to the cross to die for us, and shed His blood to redeem us from our sins. After He accomplished His redemptive work, that is, after His death and resurrection, He became the life-giving Spirit in resurrection. This Spirit is the Savior in whom we believe. Therefore, our Lord Jesus is not only the Savior and the Redeemer, but He is also the life-giving Spirit.

In Christianity today this point is greatly ignored. Today's Christianity mainly tells us how the Lord Jesus is God, how He became a man, died on the cross, washed away our sins, became our Savior, ascended into the heavens, and sat down at the right hand of the Father, and how now He is in the heavens as the object of our worship. They almost completely ignore the other half of the ministry of Jesus Christ, which is that after the Lord Jesus died and rose, He became the life-giving Spirit. First Corinthians 15:45b tells us that the last Adam, the Lord Jesus our Savior, became a life-giving Spirit. This Spirit has also come into our spirit. Therefore, 1 Corinthians 6:17 says that we have become one spirit with the Lord. Within us there truly is the fact that the two spirits are mingled as one spirit. Second Timothy 1:7 says, "God has not given us a spirit of cowardice, but of power and of love and of sobermindedness." In 2 Timothy 4:22 Paul says, "The Lord be with your spirit." This implies that the Lord is Spirit; otherwise, He could not be able to enter our spirit and be with our spirit. This again proves that the Lord Spirit has become one spirit with our spirit.

The highest Christian life is a life of the two spirits becoming one spirit. This surpasses ethics and morality. Today you and I do not merely have a conscience, the innate knowledge of good and the innate ability to do good, or the bright virtue, nor do we only have a created spirit. Within our created spirit we also have the Spirit of God, who is our Redeemer and who became the life-giving Spirit. Today I want to help everyone to practice living by this mingled spirit, that is, to practice being one spirit with the Lord. Your being saved is not just a matter of your sins being forgiven, your being cleansed by the blood, or your being redeemed and regenerated. More than that, the Lord as the Spirit has entered your regenerated spirit and mingled with your regenerated spirit to become one spirit. This is the most precious point.

There are many brothers and sisters among us who have been saved for decades. They love the Lord, and they read the Bible and pray, but their experience of the Lord remains the same as it was forty or fifty years ago. This may be compared to a person living today in the age of the jet airplane but still using an old-fashioned ox cart. The Lord has already shown us that He is with our spirit and that our spirit is one spirit with Him, but some people today, thinking that their old "ox" is not strong enough to pull well, plan to get a bigger ox to pull their cart; while everyone is flying in a jumbo jet, they are looking for a bigger ox. Today the Spirit of the Lord is in your spirit. This is clear enough, and we must practice and exercise according to this.

EXERCISING TO BE ONE SPIRIT WITH THE LORD

The condition of our spirit is completely dependent on our exercise. Even I myself up to today condemn myself for not exercising enough in this matter. We must know that we humans are not simple. We have a biological aspect and a psychological aspect. The biological aspect is our body, and the psychological aspect is our soul. Our soul, too, is very complicated; it is composed of the mind, emotions, and will. We can use three circles to illustrate this. The outermost circle is the body, the middle circle is the soul, and the innermost circle is the spirit. Man has three parts: spirit, soul, and body. For example, to become angry and hit someone is a two-layered operation. One layer is the soul getting angry, and the other layer is the hand, which is a part of the body, hitting someone in cooperation with the soul. Many people think that one cannot commit sin without the cooperation of the body. However, one can commit sin solely in the realm of the human mind. For example, one does not need to use the body to hate others. To curse others, however, requires the use of the body because one must move his mouth and tongue. Thus, when the soul and the body function together, the result is that people commit sin. For this reason, we must be delivered from the bothering of the soul, and we must exercise our spirit in the Spirit that we may become one spirit with the Lord.

Since the Lord is mingled with our spirit, and the two spirits have become one spirit, how do we need to exercise? We need to exercise in all our daily living and actions that the body will not be our starting point nor will the soul be our consideration, but that the spirit will be our center. We need to exercise according to this spirit. Are you going to argue with your wife? You must do it according to the spirit. Are you going to be angry? You must be angry according to the spirit. Some may then say that once we are according to the spirit, we will neither argue nor be angry; this is right. To be according to the spirit is simply to exercise the spirit.

In the preceding chapter, we fellowshipped about walking according to the spirit. I told you that the word *walk* in Greek means to live and walk. You have to exercise your spirit when you are angry and want to argue, but even in your ordinary speaking to others, you should stop for a minute and speak from your spirit. When you speak in the meetings, even more you must be according to the spirit; you must exercise your spirit and speak from your spirit. Once you are according to the spirit, the words that you speak will have a different flavor; therefore, you must learn how to speak from your spirit. As one who speaks for the Lord, I often practice this. My desire is that every sentence I speak will come out from my spirit. We all must confess that our exercise is still not adequate or perfect because we are still in the habit of speaking and acting according to our soul and ourselves.

EXERCISING TO WALK ACCORDING TO THE SPIRIT IN THE MEETINGS

When we all meet together, if someone merely sits quietly and does not open his mouth to testify or pray, then he will not be able to enjoy the rich supply of the Lord in the meeting. On the contrary, as long as you open your mouth in the meeting to testify, pray, or pray-read the Bible, you will be able to gain the enjoyment. If you do not open your mouth, you will have nothing, but as soon as you open your mouth, you will be supplied inwardly. When you come to the meeting, if you do nothing but come only to listen to others speak a message, what you gain will not be rich, even though your coming is better than not coming to the meeting at all. However, if you are willing to open your mouth in the meetings by praying, singing, pray-singing, pray-reading, or testifying, when you go home you will feel rich inwardly, and what you gain will be different. If I never open my mouth in the meetings that I attend, I will definitely be poor, weak, and cold. I will not have the inward watering.

Coming to the meetings is like coming to a basketball game to play and not to watch. We come not to watch the meeting but to meet. When a ball player gets onto the court, his entire being is active. Likewise, when we come to the meetings, we must use and exercise our spirit. When we come to the meetings, we are coming to worship, praise, enjoy, glorify, and exalt the Lord, so we cannot simply sit quietly. If we come to the meetings with our Bibles and hymnals, and after singing a hymn we all sit silently and no one says a word, how would you feel? I come to the meetings, and you also come to the meetings. When I come to the meetings, there are things that I should do, and when you come to the meetings, there are things that you should do. If, however, I am always the only one speaking and you are never active, then it is as if I were the only one playing in the game. The rest of you are like the other four players who do nothing but stand there, waiting for me to run over and catch the ball even when it falls right in front of you. After catching the ball, I make the play, but after everything is over, you still have not moved. This should not be our situation.

When we come to the meetings, if we do not praise or speak something to exalt the Lord or glorify Him, but we only sit there quietly, we offend the Lord. This is the condition of degraded Christianity. This is why Christianity has no way except to set up seminaries to train a group of professionals to take care of the meetings. Eventually we believers do not need to say it, for the unbelievers will say it for us: "If you have a lawsuit, find a lawyer; if you are sick, find a doctor; if you want prayer or preaching, find a pastor." We must not have such a situation among us. Among us we should not have the "leading ones" doing the tasks of the "pastors"; this is the influence of the Nicolaitans, and it is something we absolutely must overthrow. According to the revelation of the Bible, we all are priests; we were bought by the Lord with His blood to be priests (Rev. 1:5-6). Hence, everyone is a priest in the church. It does not matter if a person is young or old; as long as he has been saved and regenerated, he is a priest of God. This is just as in a family, where the husband, the wife, and the children all fulfill their duty. The husband works to earn money to support the family; the wife takes care of the household chores and serves in all the small affairs; and the children help clean the house. Everyone in the family is actively working for the household. In the same way, we are in the church our home, and we all should be active whether we are young or old. When we come to the meetings, we should each fulfill our responsibility. This will make the meetings living. When the meetings are living, they are rich. Our body is the same. When the body is active, it is healthy.

I hope that our concept and spirit will be changed. In the meetings we must use our spirit. Whenever we use our spirit, we can do many things. I do not believe that you do not contact or experience the Lord the entire week. I believe that you have at least a little experience you can speak about. Do not tell stories or speak your history. You simply need to fellowship the point that you experienced, and it will benefit the entire meeting. Do not bemoan the fact that you can speak only one point and cannot speak a long message. Actually, every point is valuable. The water that we drink is made up of many drops of water collected together. It is too poor that we appoint a brother to give a message every Lord's Day. Everyone has a portion, and if everyone brings out his portion, the entire meeting will be enriched. I hope that we will do our best to practice this.

The church is not made up of a group of people living in themselves. Whenever we live in ourselves, we are not the church. Only those living in spirit are the church. If there is Spirit, then there is the church; if there is no Spirit, there is no church. If we want the Spirit, we must exercise our spirit. We must learn this lesson. Whenever I speak, I wait at least one second and speak slowly. I have truly learned this secret. Sometimes if you had waited half a minute before speaking, you would not have said what you said. Some sisters very much like to go shopping. When you want to go shopping, you must learn not to make a hasty decision but wait for half a minute to return to your spirit. Once you are in your spirit, you may not go shopping. You must learn to exercise your spirit to first put your body aside and then to stop your soul, including the mind, emotion, and will, for half a minute so that you can return to your spirit and contact the Lord. When you turn to your spirit in this way, you are exercising your spirit, initiating from your spirit, and living and walking from your spirit. By doing this, you will find that your whole experience is totally different, as different as heaven is from earth. If we truly live in spirit, our living will be heavenly; but if we live in ourselves, our living will be earthly. There is a very great difference between the two.

CHAPTER SIX

PRAY-READING THE WORD WITH OUR SPIRIT

Scripture Reading: Matt 4:4; 2 Tim. 3:15-17; John 6:63; Eph. 6:17-18a

GOD'S MEANS TO ACCOMPLISH HIS HEART'S DESIRE

The Bible shows us that God's basic desire concerning us is to work Himself into us to be our life, our life supply, and even our enjoyment that we may be full and satisfied so that He may live Himself out of us and be expressed through us.

However, for God to work Himself thus into us to be our life and life supply, two means are necessary. Our God is great and holy, and He is also very mysterious. On our side we contact Him daily and receive Him into us as our life, our life supply, and our enjoyment, while on God's side He works Himself into us. The Bible tells us that it is through His Word and His Spirit that God is able to work Himself into us to be our life and our life supply. God gave us two exceedingly great gifts: the first is God's Word, and the second is God's Spirit.

THE WORD OF GOD

The word of God is the Holy Bible. The Bible, which is the word of God, is given to us by God as an exceedingly great gift. The word of God is not abstract at all; it has been written out and solidly put into our hands, and we can read it every day. Not only so, we can also ruminate, consider, and even research the word of God. However, we must not imagine wild things about it with our mind. Rather, our thoughts must center around the words of the Bible. We should fix our mind on the words of the Bible, digest the words of the Bible, and masticate the words of the Bible. In this manner at the very

least we will have touched the revelation of God and His
expressed desire.

We may illustrate this as follows. This morning you may
want to contact me, and I also may want to get in touch with
you. However, you may sit there silently, and I may stand
here mutely, neither of us speaking a word. If after an hour
and a half of silence we walk away from each other, we will
have received nothing. Nothing from me got into you, and
nothing from you got into me. We know that it is through
speaking that we contact each other and flow into each other.
Sometimes we also have to use our eyes to convey our feelings. When you look at me and I look at you, we can
understand each other. When you see me laugh, you know
that I am happy, and when I see you shed tears, I know that
you are sad. However, no matter how much we convey
through our eyes, we still may not know the real situation.
Therefore, we still need to talk to each other. I need to ask
you, "Why are you shedding tears? Tell me about it." When
you talk to me, your story gets into me, and I receive your
view. Your elucidation and explanation are a revelation. After
your speaking, I see your side of the story. Then I know that
you were, perhaps, wrongly accused by your father this morning. At the same time I also understand why you do not shed
tears in front of people on the street; rather, you shed tears
before me because you know that I can show a little concern
and sympathy for you. In other words, you have a place to
pour out your feelings. This makes me understand why you
are shedding tears. However, this is only a revelation; you
still cannot come into me. Although I may say a word to
comfort you that you may also have my view, I still have no
way to enter into you.

THE SPIRIT OF GOD

If God gave us merely His Word, we could understand only
His intention and at the most know His revelation, but He
could not enter into us. Therefore, He must take the second
step, that is, He must become the Spirit. I have repeatedly
said that in order to redeem us the Lord Jesus was incarnated; He put on a body of flesh and blood, and then on the

cross He died for us, suffered the judgment of God, and shed His precious blood to redeem us from our sins. After He accomplished the work of redemption, He resurrected from the dead and became the life-giving Spirit. First Corinthians 15:45b says, "The last Adam became a life-giving Spirit." When we believe in Him, confess our sins, and receive Him as our Savior, He as the life-giving Spirit enters into us. This truly is a mysterious matter.

In Greek the word for *spirit* is *pneuma,* which can also be translated as *breath.* After His death and resurrection, the Lord Jesus became the Spirit, and this Spirit is breath. In this point the Chinese language is very meaningful. When someone dies, we do not like to say that he died, but we say that he expired, that is, he breathed his last breath. To expire is to have no more breath, and to have no more breath is to have no life. Therefore, John 6:63 says, "It is the Spirit who gives life." In this verse life is connected with the Spirit. The Spirit of life is the breath of life. Breath is spirit, and spirit is breath. Our Savior Jesus is God who became a man to be our Savior. However, He did not stop there. Instead, He died and resurrected, and in resurrection He is the Spirit of life, the breath of life. Therefore, He said, "The words which I have spoken to you are spirit and are life" (v. 63b). Here, spirit and life are put together again. That which is spirit is life. This means that spirit, breath, and life are all one. If we do not have breath, we do not have life. Our physical body can illustrate this. Sometimes when we are sick, we may feel that we are short of breath. In the hospital patients who are short of breath are given oxygen. Another example is that when a car tire does not have sufficient air, it needs to be taken to the gas station and pumped up. Similarly, when our body is short of breath, we need to go to the hospital to be "pumped up."

CHRIST BEING THE WORD AND THE SPIRIT

We have to see that God, who is our Lord, not only speaks to us but also breathes into us. The Gospel of John has twenty-one chapters. The first chapter says that in the beginning was the Word and the Word was God. The Word is the Lord Himself. The Lord is the Word; He is the Word of God.

On the surface the Bible contains stories, histories, rebukes, warnings, convictions, and teachings. However, in reading the Bible you get not only these things. What you obtain is Christ. If you do not gain Christ after reading the Scriptures, then you have read in vain. We read the Bible to get Christ into us.

The Bible is the word of God, and Christ is the living word of God. The Gospel of John first tells us that Christ is the Word. Then it tells us that this Christ who is the Word became flesh, lived on the earth for thirty-three and a half years, and eventually was crucified. John 19 tells us that blood and water flowed out from His side while He was on the cross (v. 34). Blood signifies redemption, which solves the problem of our sin. Water signifies the Spirit as living water for us to receive life. Through His death, Christ accomplished redemption, signified by the blood, and He flowed out the Spirit as living water to supply man with life.

After He accomplished these things, He resurrected in chapter twenty. In the evening of the day of His resurrection He came back and stood in the midst of His disciples. His coming back at this time was different from the previous times. Previously, before His crucifixion, He was in the flesh; now, after His resurrection, He is a Spirit. He came as the Spirit to the disciples when they met together. They had shut the doors and windows tightly for fear of the persecution of the Jews. The Lord Jesus did not even knock, and no one opened the door, but suddenly the Lord stood in their midst. Therefore, they were puzzled and thought that it might be a ghost. However, the Lord came with His resurrected body and breathed into the disciples, saying, "Receive the Holy Spirit." Therefore, the Gospel of John begins by telling us that the Lord is the Word who existed from the beginning, and at the end it tells us that the Lord is the breath, the Spirit. In chapter one the Lord is the Word, whereas in chapter twenty He is the Spirit. First is the Word and then the Spirit, and in the middle of the book there is John 6:63, which says, "It is the Spirit who gives life;...the words which I have spoken to you are spirit and are life." In the beginning of the Gospel of John is the Word, at the end is the Spirit, and in between are the word and the spirit. It is the Spirit who gives life, who causes people to have life. The words which the Lord spoke to us are spirit and are life. If there were only the Word, there would be only the expression of intention; if there were no Spirit, the Lord could not come into us. Thank the Lord, we now have the Word and the Spirit.

These three—the Lord, the Word, and the Spirit—are one. The Lord is the Word, and He is also the Spirit. The Word is the Spirit, and the Spirit is the Lord. Therefore, these three are just one. John 6:63 says, "The words which I have spoken to you are spirit." Many Christians admit that the words of the Lord are the Spirit, but they have a hard time believing that the Spirit is the word. Ephesians 6:17 says, "And receive the helmet of salvation and the sword of the Spirit, which Spirit is the word of God." The word is the Spirit, and the Spirit is the word. John 6:63 says that the word is the Spirit, whereas Ephesians 6:17 says that the Spirit is the word. According to John 1:1, "In the beginning was the Word...and the Word was God." Thus the Lord is the Word. Then in 20:22 the Lord came and breathed into the disciples, saying to them, "Receive the Holy Spirit." The breath which the Lord breathed was the Holy Spirit; this proves that the Lord is that Spirit. Furthermore, there are two other places in the Bible which say that the Lord is the Spirit. First Corinthians 15:45b says, "The last Adam became a life-giving Spirit," and 2 Corinthians 3:17 says, "The Lord is the Spirit." Therefore these three verses, John 6:63, Ephesians 6:17, and 2 Corinthians 3:17, show us that the Lord, the Word, and the Spirit are all one. This is for the Lord to work Himself into us.

EXERCISING OUR SPIRIT
TO TAKE IN THE WORD OF GOD

According to the verses mentioned above, we know that the Lord is God, the Word is God, and the Spirit is God. Therefore, God, the Lord, the Word, and the Spirit are one. In order to come into us, this God who is the Lord has to be the Word and the Spirit. Ephesians 6:18 says, "By means of all prayer and petition." Prayer and petition are the ways for us to take in the word of God. This may be compared to a meal that has been prepared and set on the table by your mother. All that is needed is that you come and take it in. The best way for you to take in, to receive, a meal is to eat it. You do not come to look at the food or to study the food; you come to eat the food. The parents know very well that many times children who are naughty and disobedient just sit at the table refusing to eat the food, instead only looking at it. Moreover, there are some nutritionists who specialize in studying food, but they themselves do not eat well. Likewise, although there is only one Bible, its readers read it differently. Dr. Hu Shih read the Bible in the way of research, so he could see the Bible only as a literary work of high quality. Many Christians in reading the Bible do not come to eat but only to look; hence, they get nothing.

I hope that we all will realize that the Bible is not for us merely to research, just as a meal is not for us to research but to eat. When you eat the food, you receive the food, and as a result you gain the food. Therefore, in Ephesians 6 Paul referred to the Spirit and to the word of God. He said that you have to receive the sword of the Spirit, which Spirit is the word of God. Here he spoke of the Spirit and the word as one. Most Bible readers understand the sword of the Spirit to be the word of God. When I was young I also was taught in this way and accordingly thought that the word of God is the sword. However, here it does not say that the word of God is the sword; it says that the Spirit is the word of God. Actually, if the word of God were not the Spirit, it could not be the sword but merely words, doctrines, or black letters on white paper. The word of God must be the Spirit, and it must be living; then it can be the sword.

Paul took in, received, the word of God by means of all prayer and petition. He not only prayed in a general way, but he also petitioned in a particular way. Prayer is general, while petition is particular. Not only so, Paul prayed with "all prayer and petition." *All* includes a great number of ways. You can pray loudly, or you can pray softly. You can pray quickly, or you can pray slowly. You can pray-read not only in one way but in many ways: by yourself, with your spouse, with a group, and in the meetings. Paul said that we should receive the sword of the Spirit, the word of God, by means of all prayer and petition. This tells us that we pray all prayer and petition to take in, receive, the word of God. We come to the word of God neither to look nor to study but to take and receive it into us.

John 3:16 says, "For God so loved the world that He gave His only begotten Son, that every one who believes into Him would not perish, but would have eternal life." If you merely look at or read this verse, you may not receive anything, even though you read it ten times. Recently my two grandchildren came to see me. Their mother taught them to recite John 3:16 both in English and in Chinese. They recited very quickly, "For God so loved the world that He gave His only begotten Son, that every one who believes into Him would not perish, but would have eternal life." After listening to them, however, I thought to myself, "You are two foolish children; you have not received anything." They not only read it but also memorized it, but they did not receive it. Therefore, John 3:16 still has nothing to do with them. On the other hand, I have taken in this verse for almost sixty years. It was this verse, John 3:16, that strengthened my faith to know that I was saved. At that time, I not only read and studied this verse; in fact I pray-read it, although I did not know what pray-reading was and had never even heard the term.

I still remember that day. I was not yet very clear about my salvation, and I felt that I should read John 3:16. At first I was only reading it, and then gradually I turned from reading to receiving. I read that "God so loved the world," so I prayed, "O God, I thank You that You so loved the world." Then I prayed again, "O God, I thank You that You loved me because I am one who is of the world. O God, thank You. You so loved me so much that You gave me Your only begotten Son." At the beginning I read the verse in its original wording, but eventually I began to take it in. Once I began to take it in, the tone of my prayer changed and the pronouns changed. I prayed, "I thank You, O God, that You so loved me and gave Your only begotten Son to me, so that by believing into Him I would not perish but would have eternal life."

Although it has been nearly sixty years, I still remember

that scene very clearly. I was not only happy within, but I was full of confidence to declare to the heavens, the earth, and all things, including Satan, "I have eternal life because John 3:16 says so." This is to receive and apply the word of God. At that time nobody taught me and I did not know what pray-reading was, but I spontaneously was pray-reading without knowing it. Not only did I pray-read by myself, but I even taught others to pray-read whenever I preached the gospel. I told people, "May we read John 3:16? I will read it together with you." While we were reading, I helped them to pray-read. In this way some of them were brought in. This is to take in the word of God and the Spirit of God by pray-reading.

GOD BREATHING OUT AND WE BREATHING IN

The word of God is put before us, and its substance is the Spirit. Therefore, 2 Timothy 3:16 says, "All Scripture is God-breathed." On God's side, the Scripture is His breathing out; on our side, it is for us to breathe in. God has already breathed out. The Bible is God's breathing out, and to this day it is still God's breathing out. Therefore, whenever you come to read the Bible, if you just read the dead letters and do not breathe in what God has breathed out, then the Bible will be dead letters to you. The Scripture is the breathing out of God, whereas our prayer is our breathing in. By this breathing out and breathing in, we breathe God into us. This is the meaning of the Scriptures. However, no matter how God breathes out, if we do not breathe in, we cannot receive God as our enjoyment and supply. This is why many people come to the Bible but do not receive the life in it.

The words of the Bible are the breathing out of God, but when you turn them into prayer, they become your breathing in. Every word of the entire Scripture is the breathing out of God. How can you receive into you what God has breathed out? It is by praying the words of the Scriptures. Once you turn the words of the Bible into prayer, God's breathing out becomes your breathing in. What you breathe in is spirit and life. Therefore, the Lord said that the words which He has spoken to us are spirit and life. When the Lord's words are spirit to us, they are also life.

Thank the Lord, many of our older brothers and sisters love the Bible, which I also love. In my fifty-eight years' experience of reading the Bible I have learned a secret; that is, the most profitable way of reading the Bible is to pray-read. If you simply read in an ordinary way, "In the beginning God created the heavens and the earth," this may be profitable, yet it is merely a revelation to let you know that the heavens and the earth were created by God, that is, to let you know their origin. However, this is only knowledge; you have not gained any supply and nourishment from it. In Matthew 4 the Lord Jesus said, "Man shall not live on bread alone, but on every word that proceeds out through the mouth of God" (v. 4). Every word that proceeds out through the mouth of God is the Scriptures. In Matthew 4 the Lord Jesus dealt with the three temptations of the devil by quoting the words of the Scriptures. The Lord said, "Every word that proceeds out through the mouth of God," referring to the holy Scriptures. From the first verse to the last verse of the sixty-six books of the Bible, every word is a word that proceeds out of the mouth of God. This corresponds with 2 Timothy 3:16, which says that "all Scripture is God-breathed." The words that proceed out through the mouth of God are God's breathing out. It is not enough for us just to read and to understand what God breathed out, because then it would be mere knowledge, revelation, and doctrine. Although these are profitable to us in saving us from being ignorant, we still cannot gain the nourishment. How can we gain the nourishment from the words of the Scriptures? It is by turning these words into prayer. This is pray-reading, which is different from mere reading.

The Holy Bible is the word of God, and we live on every word that proceeds out through the mouth of God. Therefore, the Bible also tells us that God's word is our food. John 6 clearly tells us that the words which the Lord has spoken to us are life (v. 63). In verse 35 the Lord Jesus said, "I am the bread of life; he who comes to Me shall by no means hunger." He also said, "He who eats Me, he also shall live because of Me" (v. 57). Because of His concern at that time that the disciples who listened to Him might not understand the meaning of His words, He added the words in verse 63, "It is the Spirit who gives life; the flesh profits nothing; the words which I have spoken to you are spirit and are life." Therefore, you can see that the Lord's words are the food of life to us.

However, it is necessary not only for the food to be prepared in the kitchen and set on the table; it is also necessary that you come to eat it. If you do not eat, you will not get the nourishment. Therefore, we all must learn to do one thing. Every good, living, and strong Christian must learn to do this one thing, that is, to eat the word of life. The whole world today pays great attention to eating nutritiously; hence, the human life span has increased. There is an old Chinese saying which says that it is rare for one to live to the age of seventy. I praise and thank the Lord that now I am almost eighty years old. My secret is in eating; I eat properly every day. The result is that I have no less strength than those of you who are younger.

THE BEST WAY TO EAT CHRIST BEING TO PRAY-READ

Therefore, our conclusion is that to be a good and living Christian, one must eat every day. If you want to be strong and healthy, you have no alternative but to eat. However, do not eat in a haphazard way; you must eat properly, and you must also eat at the right time. I speak this word especially to the young people. I know that without exception you all are busy. Actually, everyone is busy; no one is sitting idle. Satan will not allow anyone to sit idle. It is needless to mention that you are going to school or doing a job; even if you do not do these things the whole day, you will still be busy. However, do not let your busyness be your excuse. Rather, you should remove the word *busy* from your human life. Young people, I advise you to save the time you spend on making telephone calls for gossiping. That will give you plenty of time for reading the Word and eating the Lord. Actually, this does not require very much time; half an hour a day is very good.

When we eat our meals, we should eat properly, not irregularly. For instance, I set a schedule to eat three times a day—breakfast, lunch, and dinner—and I stick to the schedule firmly. Likewise, when you come to eat the Lord's word, you must have a definite schedule. It should not be that you eat when you are happy, and you do not eat when you are not happy. Rather, you eat when you are happy, and you eat even when you are not happy. Furthermore, do not be selective in what you eat. You need to read the entire Bible. The best thing to do is to have a daily reading of some portions from the Old Testament and some from the New Testament in sequence. Begin with the first chapter of Genesis in the Old Testament and with the first chapter of Matthew in the New Testament. Obedient children eat whatever their mother serves, and they grow to be healthy. But those who are choosy in their eating are usually not healthy. I hope that you will receive my little word of exhortation.

I am telling you my experiences over scores of years. I am speaking to you not according to theology or to the teaching of Bible teachers. Rather, I am speaking to you according to the Word of God and from my experience. You all must know that the Word of God and the Spirit of God are two great means. God gives Himself to us by means of His Spirit and His breathing out. He breathes out and we must breathe in. We breathe in by praying. The best and surest prayer is to use the Lord's words as your prayer. You do not need to study hard as to how to pray; the entire Bible is your prayer book. You can read a sentence or a verse, and then you can pray these words. This is the best prayer.

When you pray, neither be too rigid nor always fluctuating. First you must use your spirit. Contact the Lord with your spirit, and ask Him to cleanse you with His precious blood. Whenever you contact the Lord with your spirit, you will feel the need for His blood to cleanse you. You may not feel that you have sinned, but you are still defiled because you are still in the old creation, in the flesh, and in the self. Even though we have not sinned, and even though we have not done anything wrong or thought anything wrong, we are still the flesh. Since we are the flesh, we need the cleansing of the blood. As those who are of the old creation, we are filthy. Therefore, every time you come to contact the Lord by reading His word, first you must pray, "O Lord, cleanse me with Your precious blood." The types in the Old Testament show us that whenever anyone went before God, he had to offer the sin offering and the trespass offering. Therefore, when you come to the Lord, you need to take Him as your sin offering and trespass offering, asking Him to cleanse you with His blood. Once you are cleansed, you will be enlivened in your spirit by the Spirit of the Lord.

When your spirit is made alive, you must learn not to speak according to your thought and your mind but according to your spirit. This does not mean that you do not use your mind any more. On the contrary, the more you use your spirit, the sharper your mind will be and the clearer and wiser your thoughts will become. Therefore, begin with your spirit; that is, touch the Lord from the deepest part of your being. Read and pray by means of His words. Just read and pray, pray and read, without trying too hard to be different or original or loud. When you are truly inspired, you may say, "Amen, O Lord, how good it is! How I praise You!" This kind of pray-reading will cause the word of God to be impressed into your whole being as your supply.

Paul said, "All Scripture is God-breathed and profitable for teaching, for conviction, for correction, for instruction in righteousness" (2 Tim. 3:16). When we pray-read in this way and get the Lord's words into us, some of the words become a conviction to us, some become a teaching, some correct us, and some instruct us in righteousness. As a result, we who are men of God are made complete, fully equipped for every good work. This is different from reading the books of Confucius and Mencius and accepting their teachings on ethics and morality. Rather, we pray by means of the Word of God and the Spirit of God to take in God Himself, who is in His words and in His Spirit. In this way, His words in us not only become a supply to us, but they also convict and teach us from deep within. This is the proper way to read the Lord's Word. May the Lord give us grace and strength and lead us to practice this every day.

CHAPTER SEVEN

CONTACTING THE LORD THROUGH HIS WORD

Scripture Reading: 1 Pet. 2:2; John 5:39-40; 6:63-68; 14:21, 23; Psa. 119:103, 105, 130, 147-148

Prayer: Lord, thank You for the constant cleansing of Your precious blood that we may receive mercy from You again to enter into Your word. Lord, we take You once again as our sin offering and as our trespass offering. By the precious blood that You shed as the offering, we come forward boldly before You. We ask that You open Your word to us. We ask also that You open Yourself to us, and we desire to open our whole being to You. May there be good fellowship between You and us. Lord, bring each one of us into the spirit and into Your grace. We pray that You will give us the word of grace that we may be nourished, supplied, enlightened, strengthened, and comforted within.

Lord, we beseech You to give each one of us a living word. What we need is Your word, not man's word. Our speaking can neither help nor supply life to others. Lord, only You Yourself and Your word are the source of life to man. We pray that You will supply us so that each one of us may not go home empty-handed but may receive a supply, go home fully filled, and be full of You within, full of light, full of grace, and full of peace. Lord, anoint each one of us and be with each one of us. Bless the future of every one of us, and remember our families and our undertakings. We commit all these matters into Your gracious hand. In Your victorious name we pray, Amen.

THE SALVATION OF GOD REVEALED IN THE BIBLE

I truly have a burden to show you from the Bible, the Lord's word, what the Lord's salvation is. What we have spoken in the past again and again from many sides all converges at this central point. Although many people have taken the Bible as a sacred writing, everyone reads according to his own way, so the understanding differs one from another. Much of our understanding of the Bible is natural and religious concepts. We think that as human beings existing in the universe we certainly need to worship a God who is in heaven, and then once we worship this God who is in heaven, He becomes our restriction. As a young boy I studied in an old elementary school where we had a class on "self cultivation," which was actually a religious subject. The purpose of religion is to regulate man's heart. One good thing about religion is that it regulates and restricts the human heart. Because the human heart is too wild, like a horse running wild that easily causes problems, mankind needs religion to restrict the heart.

Today I want to tell you that the salvation revealed to us in the Bible is not religion but the living God Himself. This living God is the sovereign Lord who created the heavens, the earth, and all things. The heavens, the earth, and all things did not come out of themselves but were created by God, the Creator of the heavens and the earth. In order to save us and to enter into us as our life, this God Himself came to be our salvation. Over nineteen hundred years ago, He came to this earth to be a man. He came to be born of a virgin in a manger. Then He grew up in a poor family in Nazareth of Galilee, and He passed through thirty years of human living in that poor family.

When He was thirty years of age, He went throughout the land doing the work of announcing God. He announced God to people, and He also lived out and expressed God for men to see. He worked in this way for three and a half years to announce and express God. Then He went to the cross to die for man and man's sin, shedding His precious blood to accomplish redemption. He was buried, and after three days He was resurrected from the dead. Since He was God, He possessed eternal life, against which death cannot prevail; thus, it was not possible for Him to be held by death. When He went into death, He entered voluntarily in order to accomplish redemption. After accomplishing His great redemptive work, He walked out of death and was resurrected.

In resurrection He became the life-giving Spirit. At this point, He is not only our Redeemer and our Savior, but even more He is our Lord of life. This Lord of life is the life-giving Spirit. Today, He is the Lord of the universe, our Redeemer, and our Savior. Moreover, He is the life-giving Spirit who enters into all those who believe into Him to be their life and life supply. This is the salvation revealed to us in the Bible.

This is not a religion but the living God as our redemption and our salvation. Moreover, He is the life-giving Spirit, who has entered into us to be our life. Today, this Savior not only is seated in the heavens but also lives in us. The most central revelation in the New Testament is that the Lord of the universe, who created the heavens and the earth, became our Redeemer and our Savior and that today, as the all-inclusive life-giving Spirit, He dwells in our spirit to be our life.

CHRIST BEING THE FOOD, DRINK, AND AIR TO THE BELIEVERS

However, this point has been neglected by many Christians today. Many dear Christians pay attention to the fact that our Lord Jesus is our Redeemer and our Savior. Regrettably, they neglect the fact that this Lord Jesus, who is our Redeemer and Savior, is also today the life-giving Spirit, who has entered into our spirit to be our life. Because of such negligence, I am particularly burdened to help people see from the Bible that the Lord Jesus is not only our Redeemer and Savior but that He is also the life-giving Spirit who dwells in our spirit, living with us moment by moment and supplying us unceasingly.

Since this Redeemer, this Savior, is in our spirit to be our life, we should contact Him and enjoy Him to receive His supply. The Bible uses many figures to tell us how we should contact and enjoy the Lord. First, the Bible says that this Savior of ours is food to us; as the bread that we can feed on, He can be received into us for our supply. This is like taking our meals. Meal after meal we receive the life supply into our stomach to supply the need of our entire body.

Sometimes, not understanding what we speak, some may say, "You are belittling the Lord Jesus by such a teaching. How can the Lord Jesus, who is the great Savior, become a small piece of bread to be taken into your stomach? Your words are blasphemous." Actually, they do not understand that this is not our own word but the word of the Lord Jesus in the Bible. In John 6:35 the Lord Jesus said, "I am the bread of life." Since He is the bread of life, He is to be eaten; He is edible.

We all know that, as Gentiles, the Canaanites were despised by the Jews. To the Jews the Canaanites were like dogs. One day when the Lord Jesus was proclaiming God on the earth to carry out God's salvation, a Canaanite woman came to seek help from Him. The Lord said, "It is not good to take the children's bread and throw it to the little dogs" (Matt. 15:26). The children are the Jews, who are God's chosen people. The bread of the children no doubt refers to the Lord Himself. The Lord came as the bread of life to be enjoyed by God's chosen people.

The Lord said that it is not good to take the children's bread and throw it to the dogs. This word indicates that not only the Jews considered the Canaanites as dogs, but even the Lord Jesus, figuratively speaking, likened this Canaanite woman to a dog. The Lord seemed to be saying: "You, who are a Canaanite dog, are trying to take a bite of Me, but I am the bread for the children, not for you." However, this Canaanite woman answered very wonderfully. She said, "Yes, Lord, for even the little dogs eat of the crumbs which fall from their masters' table" (v. 27). This is very meaningful. How can the bread become the crumbs under the table? Because the naughty children are unruly and disorderly, when they eat their meal, the food they are eating goes under the table instead of getting into their stomach. Therefore, what the Canaanite woman meant was, "Lord, I am neither a chosen one of God nor a child of God. Consider me then as a dog. The dogs also have their portion; the things on top of the table are the children's portion, whereas the things under the table are the dogs' portion. If the children eat the bread on top of the table, then as a dog can I not eat the crumbs that are under the table?" When the Lord heard this, He was moved. This answer touched His heart. Hence, He immediately did something for her and was gracious to her.

This is what I have been speaking all these years. Some people, not having seen this light in the Bible have criticized, saying, "You liken the Lord Jesus to a small piece of bread. Such a teaching is a blasphemy to the Lord Jesus!" Actually, the Lord Jesus is not only great but also small. He is both the greatest and the smallest wonderful One. In Christianity, there is a famous hymn that says, "How marvelous! How great Thou art!" Although that is a very good hymn, there is the need to write another hymn that says, "How marvelous! How small Thou art!" If the Lord were not small, He could not be eaten and get into us. Anything that can be eaten must be small. The Lord is small in order to enter into man to be man's life and life supply.

Upon hearing this word, the faultfinders might say, "You see, according to what they say, the Lord Jesus is so much smaller than they are, and they are bigger than the Lord Jesus." Today we are not here to argue but just to let all men see that when the Bible speaks of the Lord Jesus as our supply within, it uses all kinds of words and parables. The Bible says that He is the tree of life to be food for man to eat; it says that He is also the living water to be water for man to drink. The Lord Jesus Himself told the Samaritan woman, "Everyone who drinks of this water shall thirst again, but whoever drinks of the water that I will give him shall by no means thirst forever" (John 4:13-14). If the criticizers hear this word, they will consider this word as altogether derogatory, since to them it makes the Lord Jesus completely worthless. This is because they do not know how much it pleases the Lord Jesus to be the spiritual food to the believers and to supply them within. It is for this reason the Lord Jesus spoke using so many figures.

The Lord Jesus came into the midst of His disciples on the night of His resurrection and breathed into them, saying, "Receive the Holy Spirit" (John 20:22). The word *Spirit* in Greek is *pneuma,* meaning breath. Therefore, *Receive the Holy Spirit* can also be translated as *Receive the Holy Breath.*

This means that the breath which the Lord breathed is the Spirit. This indicates that in the Gospel of John the Lord Jesus is our bread, our food, our living water, and also our spiritual air.

According to our physical body, we have three great necessities in order to live: food, water, and air. Without taking any food, a person will die in eight days; without drinking water, he will die in three days. However, without breathing in air, he will be finished in only five minutes. Therefore, if a person wants to die quickly, the best way is to stop breathing. However, it is hard to stop breathing because God created man in such a way that it is hard for him to stop breathing. To breathe or not to breathe is not up to you. You have to breathe even if you do not want to. Therefore physically, man must breathe, and of course he also needs to drink and eat for his existence.

Likewise, for our spiritual life we need the Lord Jesus to be our food, our living water, and even the more, our air. All these are figures of speech, using physical and visible things to describe the spiritual and invisible reality. The Lord Jesus is our spiritual life, food, drink, and air; we cannot be separated from Him even for one moment. If we leave Him for only five minutes, we will die. Because of this, in the Gospel of John the Lord Jesus told us repeatedly, "Abide in Me and I in you" (15:4).

In 1968 I was invited to speak in Indiana, and my topic was on our abiding in the Lord and the Lord's abiding in us. While I was speaking, one sister rose up to interrupt me, saying, "Please tell me, how can we abide in the Lord, and how can the Lord abide in us?" I replied, "Physically, we are living in air, and air is also living in us. This is why we are alive. In like manner, today the Lord is the Spirit, the *pneuma,* that is, the breath. He abides in us, and we also abide in Him. It is thus we have breath and life and thereby live."

THE TWO GREAT GIFTS OF GOD—
THE HOLY WORD AND THE HOLY SPIRIT

The words which God has spoken to us throughout the ages have become the holy Word today in our hands. The Bible is not just a sacred book, but even more it is God's breathing out (2 Tim. 3:16). Every word in the Bible was breathed out from the mouth of God. All these words are living; they are spirit and are life. Furthermore, when we the believers in the Lord confess our sins and pray, calling on the Lord Jesus, and when we thus believe in Him and receive Him, He lives in us as our Savior. At this time, as the life-giving Spirit, He enters into our spirit. Therefore, we not only have the holy Word in our hand, but we also have the life-giving Spirit within us. These are truly two great gifts that God has given us.

CONTACTING THE LORD'S WORD BY THE SPIRIT

We have the holy Word in our hand and the Holy Spirit in our spirit. The Word without and the Spirit within are joined together. Therefore, the only way for us believers to contact and enjoy the Lord is to read the word of the Lord by the spirit. When we read the Bible by the spirit, we touch the Lord. This is not the way a person reads the printed pages of a book with his mind; that kind of reading cannot give us the life supply. Before we open the Bible, we must have in us an attitude of hunger and thirst for the Lord, and we should pray, "Lord, I love You, I want You, and I hunger and thirst after You. Lord, I am hungry and thirsty within, and I long to be satisfied." If we pray this way and then come to read the Bible, our emphasis will be not on our mental understanding but on our being satisfied in spirit.

Psalm 119:147 says, "I anticipated the dawn and cried out; / I hoped in Your words." The psalmist cried and hoped, hungering and thirsting within for the Lord before reading His word. In like manner, before we read the Bible, we should also spontaneously have hope. Every day when I wake up, sometimes even before I wash, I pray, "Lord, I long for You and I love You. Before I do anything, I want to receive Your supply." This is to cry and hope before the dawn. The psalmist anticipated the dawn to read the Lord's word. The psalmist was an early riser, and he was also hungry and thirsty for the Lord within. This was why he cried, hoped, and anticipated the daybreak in order to read the Lord's word. When such a person opens the Bible, he will receive a supply regardless of which verse he reads. The words of life have a positive side and a negative side. Both sides can be a supply, depending on whether or not your heart and spirit hunger and thirst for the Lord. If you hunger and thirst for the Lord, then when you come to the Bible, the words in the Bible will be to you not mere letters of an outward sacred book but rather spiritual and living words. Thus, you will spontaneously utter a prayer to the Lord. When you pray, the words of the Bible immediately enter into you. When the words of life enter into you, they become Spirit. This Spirit is life, and this life is also the supply.

CONTACTING THE LORD THROUGH HIS WORD

Do you want to live with the Lord and enjoy the Lord's life? Then you need to contact the Lord through His Word. If you would read the Bible in this way every morning, always contacting the Lord through His Word, what you will gain in the end is not just the word of life but even more the Lord Himself. The Lord is the Spirit, and this Spirit is hidden in the words of the Bible. The words of the Bible are a container, and the content within is the Lord Himself. Hence, if you read the printed pages with your mind, you will not be able to touch the Lord, but if you read with your spirit while crying from a hungry and thirsty heart, you will touch the Spirit in the Word. At this time, you will also spontaneously pray, and when you pray, the word will enter into your spirit to become spirit and life as your supply. In this way you will touch the Lord through His Word.

Once you contact the Lord, He immediately becomes the supply to you in your spirit. When you are weak, He supports you. When you are depressed, He uplifts you. When you are sorrowful, He makes you joyful. When you are in pain, He gives you comfort. When you are thirsty, He satisfies and waters you. If you are short of wisdom, He will become your wisdom from within. If perhaps at that very moment you have a problem that is hard to solve, and you have reached a point where you are in a dilemma, He will lead you from within. When you should advance, He will lead you to advance. When you should retreat, He will lead you to retreat. As a result, as the psalmist said, "How sweet are Your words to my taste! / Sweeter than honey to my mouth!" (Psa. 119:103). In reality, this honey is just the Lord Himself. The psalmist was able to taste the sweet Lord Himself through His word.

First Peter 2:2 says, "As newborn babes, long for the guileless milk of the word in order that by it you may grow unto salvation." This means that we, the saved people, should long for the guileless milk of the word as a newborn babe longs for milk. This milk of the word is the word of the Bible. The *milk of the word* was translated into *spiritual milk* in the Chinese Union Version. This is wrong. The word *spirit* is not in the Greek text; the Greek word used here is derived from *word*. Therefore, it is the milk of the word, referring to the milk in the Bible. This milk is not for teaching but for nourishing people. There are many nutrients in milk. When we drink milk, we are supplied with its many nutrients.

By drinking the milk of the word, we grow in our spiritual life. Among the Chinese only children drink milk; the adults do not. But among the Americans both young and old alike drink milk. Up until today, every day I drink a glass of milk in the morning and in the evening. Therefore, even though I am not a doctor and do not know so much about nutrition, I can testify that by my doing this I definitely have a healthy body. In like manner, if you want your spiritual life to be strong, you must drink the milk of the word in the morning. Then in the evening before you go to bed, even though you may be tired and your body may not be able to bear it, you can still use a few minutes to go back to the verses you read in the morning to enjoy them, spontaneously praying, "Thank You, Lord, You have the words of eternal life." In this way, you will not only sleep peacefully and sweetly, but you also will grow quickly in life. This is to contact the Lord through His word.

THE FUNCTION OF THE LORD'S WORD

In Psalm 119:103 the psalmist says, "How sweet are Your words to my taste! / Sweeter than honey to my mouth!" What an enjoyment! Because of such an enjoyment, the function is manifested. Verse 105 goes on to say, "Your word is a lamp to my feet / And a light to my path." One of the elements in the

Lord's word is light. When the Bible mentions light, it refers to the source of life. There is life only if there is light. Where there is darkness, there is death, but where there is brightness, there is life. Darkness brings in death, whereas light brings in life. The word of the Lord is a lamp unto our feet and a light unto our path, bringing life along with it that we may receive a supply within.

Then the psalmist goes on to say, "The opening of Your words gives light, / Imparting understanding to the simple" (v. 130). The Chinese Bible renders *simple* as *foolish*. The people of the world are all foolish, living all the day long in a muddled and befuddled condition. Young people are young fools, and old people are old fools; men are foolish, and women are also foolish. Only one kind of person in this world is not foolish, and this is one who eats the Lord's word. One who eats the Lord's word has the Lord's word in him, on the one hand, to be a lamp unto his feet and a light unto his path, and on the other hand, to shine over him and enlighten him, giving him understanding to apprehend what human life is— what it is to be a parent, to be a child, to fear God, and to live before men a life that is pleasing to God. This causes a foolish person to become a person of understanding. It is not surprising at all for the psalmist to say that he anticipated the dawning of the morning, cried, and hoped for the Lord's word, putting the Lord's word within himself to ponder over. All these speak of the function of the Lord's word.

Moreover, when we come to the New Testament, the Lord spoke an even more wonderful word. He said in the Gospel of John that His words are spirit and are life. When we receive the Lord's word, we receive the Lord Himself. As a result, what we get are the Spirit and life. In 14:21 He said, "He who has My commandments and keeps them, he is the one who loves Me; and he who loves Me will be loved by My Father, and I will love him and will manifest Myself to him." This manifestation is a supply. The Lord's manifestation is all our supply. When the Lord leaves, our supply becomes short. Therefore, we must have the Lord's manifestation to have His supply. To have the Lord's manifestation, we must love Him and keep His word. Furthermore, the Lord went on to say in verse 23, "If anyone loves Me, he will keep My word, and My Father will love him, and We will come to him and make an abode with him." This is not only His manifestation but even His making an abode with us. His manifestation is only for the moment, but His abiding with us is forever.

In 15:4 the Lord said, "Abide in Me and I in you." In verse 7 He changed the "I" into "My words," saying, "If you abide in Me and My words abide in you." This proves that this word is a living word, which is the Lord Himself. Thus, when the Lord abides in us, His words also abide in us. This word is sweet and shining, and it gives understanding to men. This word is God Himself manifested to us as the Spirit and life. Furthermore, this word is He Himself abiding in us to be our supply that we may enjoy all His riches. All these depend on our having a heart that loves Him and a spirit that hungers and thirsts for Him.

Every day and every moment, we need to tell the Lord, "Lord, I love You, I want You, and I want to contact You through Your Word." Then open the Bible, and whether it is morning, noon, or evening, you can contact Him and enjoy Him through His Word in this way. Even while waiting for a ride or riding in a car, you can also do some reading. In school or in the office, you can also use some free time to read a few verses. When you contact the Lord's word, just with a few words by the spirit the Lord's word will immediately enter into your spirit and touch your spirit. Then spontaneously you will pray. You may pray according to the Lord's word or turn the word into application. In any case, once you pray, your spirit will be supplied and will touch the Lord.

This is to enjoy the Lord, which is also to drink the milk of the word. This will cause you to have all kinds of supply within for you to be enlightened, to be led, and to know how to live before the Lord. As a result, your life will grow. This is the proper way to live with the Lord and enjoy the Lord's life, and this is also our normal Christian life.

CHAPTER EIGHT

SIMULTANEOUSLY SEEKING THE LORD AND HIS WORD

Scripture Reading: John 5:39-40; 6:63; Deut. 8:3; Jer. 15:16; Psa. 119:103, 105, 130

Prayer: Lord, thank You for gathering us to read Your Word together. We believe that You are in Your Word. Your Word is Your expression; Your Word is also Yourself because Your Word is spirit and life. O Lord, we worship You for giving us this environment that we could meet freely and come together before You to seek You. Lord, be with us and give us the Spirit, light, the supply of life, and the rich enjoyment.

O Lord, as we are reading Your Word, we pray that Your glory may shine on each line. Give us understanding and inward knowledge. Lord, make us hungry and thirsty so that we will not be inwardly numb or indifferent. Take away our lukewarmness that we may be burning inwardly to pursue You and to desire Your Word. Also, give us the utterance that You could speak from within us into everyone, so that each one of us can be supplied.

O Lord, speak to each one of us, and speak Your word into us to enlighten us. Thank You that the entrance of Your word gives light. O Lord, care for us by visiting each one of us, and resist the power of darkness for us. Thank You that Your blood cleanses us and defeats the enemy. We thank You for being with us, and in Your name we look to You. Amen.

THE INFLUENCE OF THE BIBLE ON HISTORY

To us the Lord's Word is not a small matter. If there were no Bible among men on earth, if there were no word of the Lord, then the entire world would fall into darkness. There was a period of time in history beginning from the end of the sixth century, about A.D. 570 when Catholicism was formally established and papal authority was set up, that the Bible was declared to be sealed. Only the pope and the so-called clergy beneath him were allowed to read the Bible. The excuse was that common people could not understand the Bible and, therefore, would easily make mistakes and suffer loss in their reading. Hence, the common people were not allowed to read the Bible.

From that time until around 1518 when Martin Luther was raised up by the Lord, there was a period of almost ten centuries. Those who study history all know that this period of time in history is called the Dark Ages, or the Middle Ages. Why is it called the Dark Ages? It is because during that period of time the Bible was sealed up. The common people could not read the Bible, and the result was that they fell into darkness.

The Bible was written first in Hebrew by the inspired Hebrew patriarchs. Because communication was difficult in ancient times, the influence of the Hebrew Old Testament was almost totally limited to the Hebrew people. Later, as communication and transportation progressed, the Hebrew Old Testament spread out to other lands. Around the year 400 B.C., the Greek culture spread all around the coasts of the Mediterranean Sea, especially in its southeastern part, and in Palestine and North Africa. Around the year 300 B.C., Jewish scholars living in Egypt began to translate the Old Testament from Hebrew into Greek; this was called the Septuagint. From that time on, the Old Testament came into existence in Greek. Without a doubt this caused the influence of the Old Testament Bible to increase among the Hellenized people.

After this the Lord Jesus came. By the end of the first century the New Testament was completed, written almost entirely in Greek. According to the studies of historians, when the Lord Jesus was on earth, He often quoted the Scriptures in His speaking, and His quotations of the Old Testament came from the Septuagint (meaning *seventy*), the Greek translation of the Old Testament. Thus, when the apostles continued writing the New Testament, they quoted the Old Testament from the Septuagint version. This spontaneously caused the revelation of the Bible to thoroughly penetrate the Greek culture. It was for this very reason that in the first two centuries, at the beginning of the church age, the Greek Gnostic philosophers brought the myths in Greek philosophy into the church. Thus, during the first two centuries and even up to the beginning of the third century, the myths in Greek philosophy invaded the church through the Greek Gnostic philosophers to the extent that many wrong and heretical things were taught concerning the person of God and the person of Christ. This created tremendous controversies within the church.

Recently, I have spent some time to study the truth of the Bible totally from the perspective of the Divine Trinity. The more I read, the more I saw that when the people of the first two or three centuries read the Bible, their scriptural studies eventually brought them into the tree of the knowledge of good and evil. Most of the people were there eating that tree. Eventually, the scholars themselves did not receive the supply of life, and they harmed many others by preventing them from obtaining the real supply of life.

READING THE BIBLE REQUIRING
THE EXERCISE OF OUR SPIRIT, SOUL, AND BODY

Many peoples and linguistic groups on earth today have the Bible in their own language. The Bible today has been translated into all kinds of languages and has entered into every nation. Thank the Lord, for this is a great matter! But we must know that it is useless to merely take the black and white printed words of the Bible and study them with only our mind. According to the Bible, man has three parts. The outer part is the body, within the body is the soul, and within the soul is the spirit (1 Thes. 5:23). The soul is the psyche that we sometimes hear of today. The most important part of the soul is the mind. Young people studying in school are being trained mainly in the functions of their mind: the understanding, memory, and use of their mind. But within man's soul, that is, within man's psyche, there is also the human spirit. The human spirit, soul, and body are the three parts of man.

As I am speaking, I believe that all of my three parts—my spirit, soul, and body—are being used. You can see my body; my mouth is moving, my hands are gesturing, and even my shoulders are moving with them. This is the activity of my body. If I did not have a body while speaking, there would be only my soul. You would hear a voice speaking without seeing a body, and you would certainly be frightened, thinking perhaps that I am a ghost. However, because I have a body while I am speaking, you need not be afraid. Moreover, if I were merely teaching at a school or making a speech, it would be enough for me to use my body and my mind, my understanding. I would not need to use my spirit. However, as I am speaking, the most important matter is my spirit. We can all tell that listening to a lesson in the classroom is one thing, while listening to a message in the meeting is another thing. The former does not require us to use our spirit, but the latter does. In the classroom, you might be touched at times to shed tears or to laugh, but these have nothing to do with your spirit. In the meetings, however, all of us, especially those of us who speak for the Lord, must have sufficient prayer and exercise to use our spirit more than our soul or outward body, because we desperately want to allow the Lord to speak His word from our spirit.

It is the same with reading the Bible. When you read the Bible, you absolutely must remember to use all three parts—spirit, soul, and body. You certainly must use your eyes and your mouth to read; this is to use your body. In Chinese, the word *read* does not mean to read silently but to read aloud. Reading the Bible should be done aloud. When we read the Bible, we first use our body, then our mind, and then our emotion. We must use our emotion to appreciate and love the Word. Why do you like to read novels? It is because your emotions tell you to keep on reading them. Why do you nod off when you read the Bible? It is because you do not appreciate it with your emotions. Therefore, you must pray and ask the Lord to cause you to desire His Word. However, this is not enough. You have used only two of your three parts, your body and soul, but you still have not used your spirit.

Our spirit is our innermost part. The best way to use our spirit is to pray with our spirit. For example, when we want to use our feet, the best way is to walk. In the same way, if we want to use our spirit today, the best way is to pray. It is very easy to gossip and to criticize others, because you do not need to use your spirit for this. All you have to do is make a telephone call, and your gossip and criticism will come out. But if you want to use your spirit, you must pray. Therefore, when you read the Bible, not only your eyes and mouth must cooperate, and not only must you use your soul to understand and love the Word, but you must also pray, expressing in prayer what you have read and understood. This prayer is the use of your spirit. In this way, you use your spirit, soul, and body, and you will not merely be touching the Bible without contacting the Lord. However, if you do not use your spirit to pray, then you may remain in a situation where you only touch the Bible without contacting the Lord. This means that you only seek Bible knowledge without seeking the Lord.

SIMULTANEOUSLY SEEKING BOTH THE LORD AND HIS WORD

We must simultaneously seek the Lord and His Word. First we need to seek the Lord. Whenever we are going to read the Scripture, even before we open the Bible, we should pray. It does not matter whether it is in the morning, in the evening, or at noontime; whenever you open the Bible, before you read the Lord's Word, you should always pray first. You do not have to follow any formalities, so you may either kneel or sit. The only thing you need to do is spontaneously express the feelings in your heart. This expression of your heart is prayer, and it is the coming forth of your spirit: "O Lord, I love You. I thank You that now I am coming to read Your Word." All it takes is a short, simple prayer like this for you to seek the Lord. Do not despise this simple practice; it is truly precious. You do not need to say the same thing every time, because it is not a matter of what you say. The point is that you pray, showing that your heart is turned to the Lord and that you are seeking the Lord.

When you pray, first seek the Lord. Then when you open the Bible to read, you will be able to inwardly understand what you are reading, and you will desire the Word. At this time, you will spontaneously turn what you have read, desired, and understood into a prayer. For example, you might read John 1:1, and perhaps you will pray, "O Lord, I praise You that You are the Word who was in the beginning. You existed from the beginning, and You are the Word of the beginning. When we breathe, we breathe You in as this Word. This Word defines God." In this way you turn the Lord's word into prayer; your prayer can be many words or just a few words. It is even all right to pray only one sentence. You can say, "O Lord, thank You that You are the Word who was in the beginning." When you turn the Lord's Word into your prayer, the Spirit comes, and at the same time you are seeking the Lord.

If you pray in this way, the Lord says that His words are spirit and life. If you do not pray like this but only open the Bible to read, then even though this Bible is the Lord's word, it is only words in black and white letters to you. The modern Chinese philosopher Mr. Hu Shih also read and studied the Bible, but he studied only with his mind and never touched the Spirit; therefore, he did not receive life. We are not like this. Whenever we read the Bible, we first pray to the Lord to open to Him that our spirit may contact Him, and then we read and are able to understand. Once we understand, we spontaneously have a desire, and then at this time we turn what we have read and desired into a prayer. Then when we pray, the words of the Bible become the Spirit and life. This is a marvelous experience!

READING THE BIBLE REQUIRING US TO USE OUR SPIRIT TO CONTACT THE LORD THAT WE MAY HAVE ETERNAL LIFE

In John 5:39-40 the Lord Jesus said, "You search the Scriptures, because you think that in them you have eternal life; and it is these that testify concerning Me. Yet you are not willing to come to Me that you may have life." It says here that the Bible is the testimony of the Lord Jesus. At the time the Lord Jesus was on earth, the Jewish teachers and leaders were zealous to search the Scriptures. They did not merely read, but they searched and studied because they thought that in the Scriptures they had eternal life. However, the Lord Jesus said, "It is these that testify concerning Me." What the Lord Jesus meant was, "You think that in the Scriptures there is eternal life, but you must know that the Scriptures speak of Me, the Christ. The reason the Scriptures have eternal life is because the contents of the Scriptures speak about Me, the Lord Jesus. Only I, the Lord Jesus, am the eternal life."

Eternal life is not what most people understand it to be, merely an eternal blessing. Eternal life is the uncreated, indestructible life of God. The Lord rebuked those Pharisees saying, "You teachers of the Jews search the Scriptures which testify concerning Me, because you think that in them you have eternal life, but you are not willing to come to Me." This proves that people can read the Bible without contacting the Lord of life. Thus, our real need is to simultaneously seek the Lord Himself and His Word.

We cannot separate the Lord from His words. If you separate the Lord from His words, you will get nothing. We must see that the Lord is the contents of His words; His words are His expression and container. The Bible is like a bottle, and the Lord Himself is like the water in the bottle. Today if you do not have the bottle, you have no way to drink the water, nor can you carry the water. Likewise, if you only hold the bottle without drinking the water, you will not get anything. If we want to enjoy the water, we must both hold the bottle and take a drink.

Our reading the Bible and seeking the Lord are just like drinking water; reading the Bible is like holding the bottle, and praying to the Lord is like drinking the water. Suppose you offer me a cup of tea, and I take that cup of tea but only look at it, saying, "This cup is the best China produced in Ching The Chen in Chiang-hsi Province, that city famous for its porcelain." If I were to admire the cup for half a day without drinking one mouthful of the tea, I would offend you. You offer me the tea, not the cup. You want me to drink the tea, not to admire your cup. It is only by drinking the tea that I can quench my thirst and honor you. This is what the Lord's word in John 5 means. He rebuked the Jewish teachers for admiring the Scriptures without being willing to touch the content of the Bible, which is the living Person, Jesus Christ, the eternally living Lord. They were studying the Scriptures because they thought that only in them they had eternal life, but they did not know that this Bible speaks of the Lord Jesus who is the eternal life. They only searched the Scriptures but were not willing to come to the Lord Jesus to obtain the eternal life.

Remember, therefore, that when you read the Bible you must contact the Lord. Do not merely read the Bible without exercising your spirit. When you read the Bible without exercising your spirit, it is the same as searching the Scriptures without coming to the Lord. If you do not come to the Lord, then all you will get is knowledge. The same Bible may be to you either knowledge or life; it all depends on whether or not you exercise your spirit to touch the Lord when you read it. The tree of life and the tree of the knowledge of good and evil are both here; it all depends on how you read. You must read the Bible with your body, understand and long for it with your soul, and pray over it with your spirit. Once you pray, you immediately touch the Lord through the holy Scriptures and obtain life.

Some people may ask, "Isn't the Lord within us? It doesn't matter whether or not we come to the Lord because He is already within us." This are right; in any event the Lord is within us, but we still need to contact Him. The Lord is in us, but we must pray to contact Him. Because the Lord as the Spirit abides in our spirit, whenever we pray, we exercise our spirit and are able to contact the Lord. However, many people are not willing to exercise in this way. They listen to a message or read the Bible, but they are not willing to pray. The result is that they only get the doctrines in black and white letters, but they do not contact the Lord. If we only get the doctrines or touch the Bible without contacting the Lord, then we have no way to obtain eternal life.

I hope that we can all correct this error by always praying before we read the Bible and by turning into prayer what we have understood in our reading. This is to seek the Lord and simultaneously seek His Word. We absolutely must not separate these two matters. Instead, we must combine our reading of the Bible with our praying, so that our reading is our praying and our praying is our reading. In this way, not only the words of the Lord will enter into us, but He also will enter into us in and with His words. As a result, not only will we obtain the Lord's words, but the Lord will be one with His words and enter into us as our supply.

In John 6:63 the Lord Jesus said, "It is the Spirit who gives life; the flesh profits nothing; the words which I have spoken to you are spirit and are life." The words, the Spirit, and life are three items, but the Lord speaks of them here as one. When the words are merely words, they are only black letters printed on the white paper; they are not the Spirit. But when the words get into your mind through your eyes and you begin to pray with your spirit, then the words become the Spirit. When the words become the Spirit, they are life.

When we pray in our reading of the Word, we turn the verses we have read into prayer. When we pray, we must forget everything else and have only the Lord and His word. *Hymns, #389* says, "From morning to evening my one world Thou art." This means that when we seek the Lord, we have only one world: "O Lord, You are my world; I seek You." When you pray a simple prayer like this, whatever you read and understand will enter into you. Once the word enters your spirit, it becomes the Spirit and life. However, if you do not pray, then the word that you read will not become the Spirit, nor will it become life.

Deuteronomy 8:3 says, "And He humbled you and let you go hungry and fed you the manna, which you had never known nor your fathers had ever known, so that He might make you know that man lives not by bread alone, but that man lives by everything that proceeds out from the mouth of Jehovah." When the Lord Jesus was being tempted in the wilderness, He quoted this verse to answer the devil (Matt. 4:4). This shows us that the words of God are not only teachings, but as the manna from heaven they are also food for our nourishment and supply. Teachings are for educating our mentality that we may have knowledge to understand and comprehend. Food does not give knowledge; it causes us to obtain an inward supply of life. Therefore, the Lord Jesus said that the words which He speaks to us are spirit and are life, that is, the supply of life.

This is why in John 6 the Lord also told us, "I am the bread of life; he who comes to Me shall by no means hunger" (v. 35). Moreover, He said, "He who eats Me, he also shall live because of Me" (v. 57). These passages show us that the Bible is not merely a book for us to receive religious teachings and obtain knowledge about God. Rather, the words in the Bible are the words that proceed out through the mouth of God. When we read the Bible, we should not only read and understand it, but we must also pray. When we pray, the words that proceed out through the mouth of God enter into our spirit. When the words enter our spirit, they are spirit and life, and they become our food as our living supply.

THE WORD OF GOD BEING THE MEANS FOR GOD TO BE OUR LIFE SUPPLY

We all know that if we ate sand and got it into our stomach, this sand cannot supply us as food does, and it will even harm our body. Because sand is not organic, it does not have any elements with which to supply us. Any food, such as meat or vegetables, is necessarily organic. Because our body is organic, our food must also be organic for us to be able to digest and assimilate it. Through the organic function of our body, the food that we eat is organically digested into our body to be our life supply so that our body may obtain life.

If you do not eat anything all day, by evening time you will feel that you have no strength. If you do not eat for seven days, you may die. Therefore, our supply of life depends upon food. In the same way, we Christians not only have physical life, but we also have life in our spirit. The life in our spirit must have God Himself as the supply. However, because God is abstract and mysterious, we must have the substantial Bible, the word of God, as the means for us to obtain the supply of God. By reading and understanding God's words and by turning what we read and understand into our prayer, the words enter into us as life to become our life supply. This is the proper way to read the Bible—considering the Lord's words as food and not as teachings or religious writings.

Thus, Jeremiah 15:16 says, "Your words were found and I ate them, / And Your word became to me / The gladness and joy of my heart." Good food always makes us happy; the Lord's words are the same. When we eat the Lord's words, we have joy and rejoicing in our hearts. Psalm 119:103 says, "How sweet are Your words to my taste (lit., palate)! / Sweeter than honey to my mouth!" This verse does not say that God's words are in my mind. If this were so, that would mean that I study them with my mentality. It says that God's words are on my palate, in my mouth. This is a description of the taste of enjoyment. One has to be very particular in eating. If one eats too quickly, gobbling things ravenously, then he will not have much sweet enjoyment.

THE FUNCTIONS OF THE LORD'S WORD

A Lamp to Our Feet and a Light to Our Path

Next, verse 105 says, "Your word is a lamp to my feet / And a light to my path." On the one hand, we should not consider the Bible to be mere teachings, but on the other hand, we still need to be taught. First, the Lord's word is our food to be our supply and enjoyment. Then, it becomes our lamp and our light to guide us. Today's society is in darkness everywhere. Schools, offices, businesses, and so forth are all in darkness. But if you carefully chew and taste the Lord's words, allowing them to be digested within you, they will shine forth to enlighten you inwardly and make you feel that in the path of human life, your every step has a lamp and is full of light.

Sixty years ago when I was still a small child, it was completely dark outside our door at night, so we had to carry lanterns outdoors and walk carefully step by step. In those days the roads were not as even as they are today. There were always little bumps and hollows. When we walked, we had to use the light and look carefully before we took a step. This was the way we walked in those days. Today in our human society, it is as if we are walking at night, as we did in the old days. Even if you are a young person in school, your way is very bumpy, and everything is in darkness. However, if you read and eat the Lord's word every day, then His word will shine brightly within you and prevent you from stumbling.

Giving Understanding to the Simple

This is why verse 130 says, "The opening of Your words gives light, / Imparting understanding to the simple." The word *opening* here does not mean the opening up of a truth through an explanation, but it refers to an actual digestion. When the Lord's words are eaten by us and digested in us, then they have an entrance and shine forth light. For example, you may often lose your temper with your wife, and the elders may exhort you with Ephesians 5:25, saying, "Husbands, love your wives." Their exhortation, however, does not have much effect because the Lord's word has not been digested within you.

If you truly digest the Lord's word, even if you do not read Ephesians 5 but instead read John 6:63, "The words which I have spoken to you are spirit and are life," immediately you will have the inward process of digestion. Once the Lord's word is digested in you, it gives forth light. You are immediately in the light, and you see that your attitude toward people is wrong. You see that not only have you lost your temper with your wife, but your attitude toward others is also inappropriate. Sometimes you seem to have the proper attitude toward others, but it is false; it is only a kind of outward politeness while you inwardly detest that person. Therefore, it is not necessary that you specifically pray-read the verses about loving your wife or submitting to your husband. The only thing you need to do is use your spirit in reading the Bible. The operation of the Lord's word is so broad that it spontaneously will enlighten you in every aspect.

EXERCISING TO READ THE BIBLE

I hope that you brothers and sisters will spend a little time every day, at least ten minutes, to read a small portion of the Lord's Word. The young people need at least ten minutes to eat a meal, but when they eat in just ten minutes, they do not digest the food very well, so it is better to use half an hour. Similarly, we should spend at least ten minutes every day, and it is best if we spend half an hour, to read the Lord's Word. Today we are all the saved children of God who have the inward spiritual life. This spiritual life needs nourishment. If you do not feed it, this life will not grow up. I have several grandchildren; all those who know how to eat are husky, and those who do not like to eat as much are skinny. I hope you all will take my word to have a good appetite every day and to spend a little time to read, understand, desire, and pray the Lord's Word. In this way you not only seek the Lord's Word but you also seek the Lord Himself.

I hope you will not take this merely as a doctrine to listen to, but rather that you will receive this word and practice it in your daily life. I hope that every day you will exercise to read the Lord's Word in this way. As to how you read, I would advise you not to pick and choose, because picky eaters who eat only their favorite foods do not grow up to be healthy. It is best to read both the New Testament and the Old Testament at the same time, starting with Matthew in the New Testament and with Genesis in the Old Testament. Read the New Testament in the morning and the Old Testament in the evening, and read straight through according to their sequence without skipping over the difficult passages. When you are reading, you must remember to pray over it verse by verse, because the Lord's words are life and truth and because this Lord is in our spirit today. We must first ask Him to cleanse us with His blood, and then we exercise our spirit to pray over what we have read and understood in His Word. In this way we will touch the Lord inwardly and receive His supply. Consequently, our entire being will be in the light of life, and this light of life will be our life supply, enlightening us and supplying us in every matter so that we will have light in our path and strength in our work.

ABOUT THE AUTHOR

Witness Lee was born in 1905 in northern China and raised in a Christian family. At age 19 he was fully captured for Christ and immediately consecrated himself to preach the gospel for the rest of his life. Early in his service, he met Watchman Nee, a renowned preacher, teacher, and writer. Witness Lee labored together with Watchman Nee under his direction. In 1934 Watchman Nee entrusted Witness Lee with the responsibility for his publication operation, called the Shanghai Gospel Bookroom.

Prior to the Communist takeover in 1949, Witness Lee was sent by Watchman Nee and his other co-workers to Taiwan to ensure that the things delivered to them by the Lord would not be lost. Watchman Nee instructed Witness Lee to continue the former's publishing operation abroad as the Taiwan Gospel Bookroom, which has been publicly recognized as the publisher of Watchman Nee's works outside China. Witness Lee's work in Taiwan manifested the Lord's abundant blessing. From a mere 350 believers, newly fled from the mainland, the churches in Taiwan grew to 20,000 in five years.

In 1962 Witness Lee felt led of the Lord to come to the United States, settling in California. During his 35 years of service in the U.S., he ministered in weekly meetings and weekend conferences, delivering several thousand spoken messages. Much of his speaking has since been published as over 400 titles. Many of these have been translated into over fourteen languages. He gave his last public conference in February 1997 at the age of 91.

He leaves behind a prolific presentation of the truth in the Bible. His major work, *Life-study of the Bible,* comprises over 25,000 pages of commentary on every book of the Bible from the perspective of the believers' enjoyment and experience of God's divine life in Christ through the Holy Spirit. Witness Lee was the chief editor of a new translation of the New Testament into Chinese called the Recovery Version and directed the translation of the same into English. The Recovery Version also appears in a number of other languages. He provided an extensive body of footnotes, outlines, and spiritual cross references. A radio broadcast of his messages can be heard on Christian radio stations in the United States. In 1965 Witness Lee founded Living Stream Ministry, a non-profit corporation, located in Anaheim, California, which officially presents his and Watchman Nee's ministry.

Witness Lee's ministry emphasizes the experience of Christ as life and the practical oneness of the believers as the Body of Christ. Stressing the importance of attending to both these matters, he led the churches under his care to grow in Christian life and function. He was unbending in his conviction that God's goal is not narrow sectarianism but the Body of Christ. In time, believers began to meet simply as the church in their localities in response to this conviction. In recent years a number of new churches have been raised up in Russia and in many eastern European countries.